AGEING IN MEGHALAYA

AGEING IN MEGHALAYA

C. Joshua Thomas
&
Fiasta T. Diengdoh

ICSSR–NERC, SHILLONG, MEGHALAYA

&

AKANSHA PUBLISHING HOUSE
NEW DELHI-110002 (INDIA)

AKANSHA PUBLISHING HOUSE
4649-B/21, Ansari Road
Darya Ganj, New Delhi - 110 002
Ph.: 23263193 / 9811582579 / 09435116718
Fax: 011-23263193
Email: ektabooks@yahoo.com
www.akanshapublishinghouse.com

Ageing in Meghalaya

First Published 2009
Reprint 2026
ISBN 978-81-8370-175-4

PRINTED IN INDIA

Published by Akansha Publishing House, New Delhi and Prin at Aryan Enterprises, Delhi.

CONTENTS

	Foreword	vii
	Preface	ix
	Acknowledgement	xiii
	Project Team	xv
	Executive Summary	xvii
1.	**Introduction**	**1-17**
	1.1 Generalities	1
	1.1.1 Elderly – Meaning of the term	8
	1.1.2 Problems of the Elderly	10
	1.2 Objectives of the Study	14
	1.3 Methodology	15
2.	**State Profile**	**18-35**
	2.1 Current scenario of Elderly person in Meghalaya	23
3.	**General Information and Status of the Elderly**	**36-45**

4. **Informal Care Givers and Financial Dependency of the Elderly** 46-66
   - 4.1 Informal Care Givers and the Welfare of the Elderly 46
   - 4.2 Financial Dependency of the Elderly 58

5. **Status of Health of the Elderly: Health Problems and Health Care Services** 67-74

6. **Social Concerns for the Elderly** 75-92
   - 6.1 Policies and Programmes of the Government of Meghalaya Towards the welfare of the elderly 76
   - 6.2 Views, Opinions and Suggestions of the Key Informants on the problems and welfare of the elderly 77
   - 6.3 Views, Opinions and Suggestions of the Headmen, Social workers (SW), Non-Governmental Organisations (NGOs) and Community workers (CW) on the Problems and welfare of the Elderly 87
   - 6.4 Opinions and suggestions of the elderly on care and support system 89

7. **Conclusion: Recommendations and Suggestions** 93-108

Bibliography 109

Annexures 114

I-Interview schedule

II-National Policy on Older Persons

III-National Programme for care of Older Persons: an update

Index 163

North-Eastern Hill University
NEHU Campus, Shillong - 793022 (Meghalaya)

Phone :
Grams : Nehu

Prof. Pramod Tandon
Vice-Chancellor &
Chairman, NERC-ICSSR

Telephone Nos.0364-2721003/4 & 255
0101 (O) 2550100/0074 (R)
FAX No. 0364- 2550076/1634
e-mail:vcnehu@nehu.ac.in
28th November, 2007

FOREWORD

I am pleased to write a foreword to this book on Ageing in Meghalaya. Ageing is a natural and universal phenomenon as it is experienced by all the societies in all generations and all countries but its magnitude and manifestations are not the same everywhere. Governments all over the world are taking special effort to alleviate problems of the aged in their respective states.

The present report on Ageing in Meghalaya has been carried out by the Indian Council of Social Science Research, North Eastern Regional Centre, Shillong, with the financial assistance from the Department of Social Welfare, Government of Meghalaya. The study apprises the magnitude of the problems of the elders in the state of Meghalaya and suggests some policy recommendations to alleviate such problems.

I wish that this book will be used to improve planning and implementation of programmes and services for the welfare of the aged in the state of Meghalaya and I compliment the ICSSR-NERC team and the Department of Social Welfare, Government of Meghalaya for this commendable work.

Pramod Tandon

Pramod Tandon

PREFACE

This book, *Ageing in Meghalaya,* is an outcome of a small sample survey carried out by the Indian Council of Social Science Research, North Eastern Regional Center (ICSSR-NERC). It was sponsored by the Department of Social Welfare, Government of Meghalaya, Shillong.

The objective of this sample survey was to assess the general profile of the elderly in the State, their socio-economic status as well as health and age-related issues. Through this exercise, it is hoped, the department will be able to formulate appropriate policy for the elderly in Meghalaya.

Data for the survey was obtained mainly through a broad questionnaire (Annexure -1) that was circulated among 231 randomly selected elderly respondents, covering seven district headquarters of Meghalaya. This was supplemented by observations, interviews and informal discussions with the respondents as well as selected Key Informants, comprising headmen, social/ community workers, NGOs and State officials concerned.

Apart from these, we have reviewed all available research, documents and articles on Ageing and issues related to the elderly population in India. We also ran through some reports published in newspapers, magazines and journals to have a better understanding of the issues.

The book, therefore, is not an exhaustive study on Ageing and the elderly population, but it clearly outlines the basic profiles of the elderly population in Meghalaya and some of its main concerns and how these may be addressed by the various stakeholders.

It is generally viewed that being a matrilineal society, in which traditional customs and values are deeply entrenched, the elderly are well looked after in Meghalaya, and so until recently, there has been little focus on the quality of life of the elderly population in Meghalaya.

This sample survey, even if it has been done on a small scale, indicates that with changing time certain problems are affecting the elderly population in Meghalaya, too, which deserve attention and mitigation.

Though Ageing is a natural phenomenon across the world, the magnitude of the problems of the elderly varies from place to place and culture to culture. Apart from concerns over deteriorating performance of the body due to the natural process of ageing, the elderly suffer from socio-psychological trauma. This is not because of changes in their temperament and attitude, but often due to society's changing attitudes towards the elderly.

The book is divided into seven brief chapters. The first chapter offers a general overview of the issues related to ageing and the elderly population and introduces the objectives and methodology of the study; the second chapter describes the State profile and the current scenario of the elderly, while the third chapter deals with the status of the State's elderly population. The fourth chapter discusses about the informal care givers and the types of the welfare schemes as well as the issue of financial dependency. The fifth chapter outlines the health problems and the status of the health care services available to the elderly. The sixth chapter articulates the social concerns for the elderly. It examines the existing state programmes for the elderly and sums up the views and suggestions of the key informants as well as the elderly respondents. The final chapter is the wrap up of the report with conclusions and recommendations for various stakeholders. For the sake of clarity we have changed the title of the report to Ageing in Meghalaya.

We sincerely believe this brief book will help stakeholders, especially the department concerned, improve their understanding of the issues concerning the elderly and formulate suitable interventions to redress them.

September 2008 **C. Joshua Thomas**
Shillong **Fiasta T. Diengdoh**

ACKNOWLEDGEMENT

The Report, ***The Magnitude of the Problem of Elderly Person in Meghalaya*** was sponsored by the Department of Social Welfare, Government of Meghalaya, Shillong. We are thankful to Shri Y Tsering, IAS, Commissioner and Secretary, Ms L Diengdoh, IAS, former Director and Shri C C M Mihsil, MCS, the present Director, Department of Social Welfare, Government of Meghalaya, for initiating and extending all help required for the project.

There are many people who contributed immensely directly and indirectly in the course of the preparation of the report, and they all deserve special thanks. We are grateful to various officials from the Census Office (Shillong), District Social Welfare (DSC), Deputy Commissioner's (DC) Office, District Rural Development Agencies (DRDA) and Block Development Office (BDO) for providing all the relevant data. The various Non-Governmental organizations (NGOs),

Headmen, Charitable organizations, prominent Community/Social workers and particularly the officials at Mercy Home deserve appreciation for the valuable information provided by them in the course of the fieldwork. Due acknowledgement is given to Prof. B S Mipun, Department of Geography, NEHU, for the support in making provision for maps. We are grateful to Dr N P Goel, Centre for Adult Education, NEHU, for his help in tabulation and interpretation of the data.

Dr Gurudas Das, Head, Department of Humanities & Social Sciences, NIT, Silchar deserves special appreciation for making necessary changes and analyzing the whole report and also assisting in the project as Consultant. We put on record the following scholars who had gone through the draft report and given their valuable comments: Dr H Srikanth, Dr Prasanjit Biswas and Dr Santanu Ray of NEHU and Ms I M Syiem of St Edmunds College. This report would not have been possible without the help and sincerity of our Research Associate Ms Donna Diengdoh and the Research Investigators, Mr Eric Nongrum and Mr Suffice Momin. We appreciate much for their ungrudging support throughout the field work.

Shri Sanat Chakraborty, Editor, *Grassroot Options*, Shillong deserves special appreciation for giving final touch to the book as the Copy Editor.

We are grateful to all our colleagues at the Centre for their cooperation and assistance. Lastly, the respondents of the present study deserve special appreciation for their kind cooperation during the interview to our investigators.

PROJECT TEAM

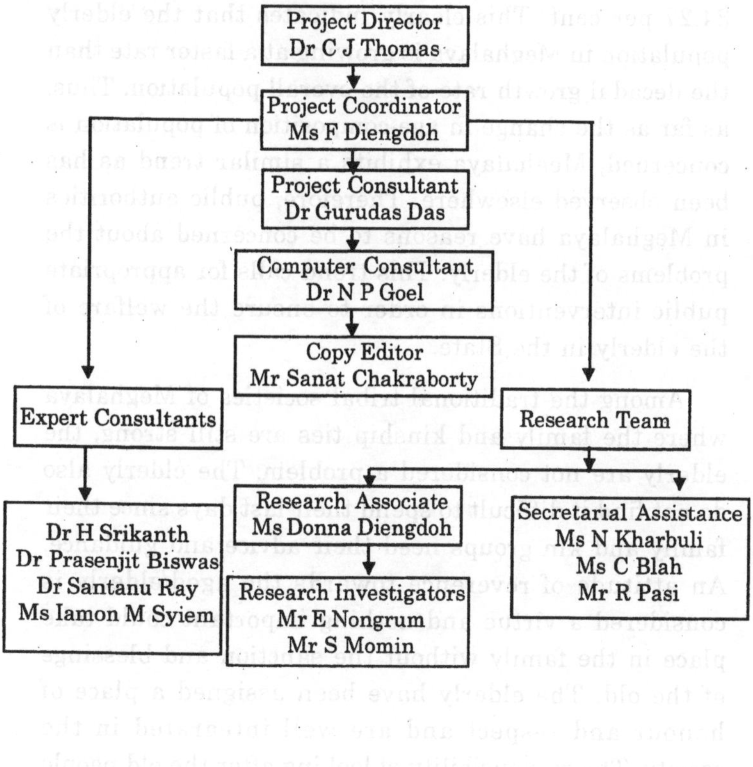

was higher than the females, in the urban areas their proportion was almost the same.

In 2001, while the population of Meghalaya went up to 2,318,822, with 50.72 per cent male and 49.28 per cent female, the total number of elderly was 1,05,726. Of the total elderly, 51.09 per cent were males and 48.91 per cent were females. A comparison between the 1991 and 2001 population census reveals that while the decadal growth rate of population in Meghalaya has been 30.65 per cent, the same for the elderly population stands at 34.27 per cent. This clearly indicates that the elderly population in Meghalaya is growing at a faster rate than the decadal growth rate of the overall population. Thus, as far as the change in age-composition of population is concerned, Meghalaya exhibits a similar trend as has been observed elsewhere. Therefore, public authorities in Meghalaya have reasons to be concerned about the problems of the elderly. This trend calls for appropriate public interventions in order to ensure the welfare of the elderly in the State.

Among the traditional tribal societies of Meghalaya where the family and kinship ties are still strong, the elderly are not considered a problem. The elderly also do not find it difficult to spend their last days since their family and kin groups need their advice and guidance. An attitude of reverence towards the aged/elderly is considered a virtue and nothing important could take place in the family without the sanction and blessings of the old. The elderly have been assigned a place of honour and respect and are well integrated in the society. The responsibility of looking after the old people is taken for granted. So the elderly too don't feel that they are useless and unwanted.

This scenario is, however, gradually changing with the deepening of forces of modernization. Traditional values are giving way to the predicaments of modern living. The informal care taking system built-in traditional social and family structures is slowly fading away. The change in social family structures is resulting in declining role and status of the elderly in the society. In this changing situation the old persons feel depressed, insecure and deprived in their family and community.

Therefore, as in other societies, the elderly population in Meghalaya too is experiencing deterioration in their status. They are probably unable to articulate their grievances, but they seem to say they are not cared. The evidences show that slowly and steadily, the elderly people in this part of the country, too, are facing major problems, which need immediate attention.

2. Key Findings

Trends in growth of elderly population

- Elderly population in Meghalaya is growing at a faster rate than the overall growth of population.
- While the decadal growth rate of population has been 30.65 per cent during 1991-2001, the same for the elderly population stands at 34.97 per cent.
- Growth of the elderly population is not evenly distributed across the state.

- Growth of the elderly population is concentrated in three districts, viz., Jaintia Hills, West Khasi Hills and East Garo Hills.
- Rural Meghalaya bears much of the burden of the elderly population than its urban counterparts.
- While in 1991, longevity at age of 60 of the females was higher than the males, this gap has been reduced in 2001.

Trends in old age financial security

- About 56 percent of the respondents have reported that they are facing financial problem.
- Elderly people face more financial problem during the early years of their retirement from active life. It is perhaps because a time lag is needed to adjust their consumption and spending habits with their reduced financial status. Financial problem is less pronounced among the people of very old age (above 75 years of age).
- In Meghalaya, the elderly males face relatively more financial problem than the females. Matrilineal social formation may be the reason for this inter-sex disparity.
- The problem of old age financial security is acute among the Garos, moderate among the Khasis and less among the Jaintias.
- It has been found that the problem of old age financial security bears some inverse relationship with the educational qualifications of the respondents. The lesser the educational

qualification, the higher is the magnitude of the problem of old age security and vice versa. It is evident that education instills skills in individual. The higher the level of education, the better is the prospect of formal jobs which fetch higher income. With formal sector jobs come old age security provisions. Moreover, higher income enables individuals to save more for the old age and thereby reduces financial dependency.

- Occupations of the elderly in their active life largely determine their status of old age security. It has been noted that 84 per cent of the elderly who were/are associated with farming face financial problem. About 56 per cent of the elderly who were/are associated with non-farming activities reported to have financial problem. The elderly females, who were/are housewife, also face considerable amount of old age financial insecurity.
- Education, occupation, income and old age financial security are all related. Better education enables an individual to find better jobs and earn higher income. The higher the level of income, the better is the financial position of an individual at old age. It has been noted that less number of respondents having higher income reported to have financial problem.
- It has, thus, been observed that the illiterates, self-employed, low-income groups are more vulnerable to old age financial insecurity than the literate and formal sector employees group of people. Old age

security measures have to be focused on this vulnerable section of the elderly.

Trends in status of health of the elderly

- About 50 per cent of the respondents reported to have health problems. It has been observed that with age health problem increases. While 44 per cent of the elderly of the age group of 60-65 have reported health problems, this percentage rises with the age and about 85 per cent of the elderly of the age group of 80 plus reported to have health problems. Thus, problem of health bears a positive relation with age. This is a general trend and Meghalaya sample shows no exception.
- Contrary to the general believe that male elderly suffer from more health problems than the female elderly maybe due to greater exposure of the former towards stress related activities and unhealthy habits like drinking, smoking, etc., higher percentage of female elderly in Meghalaya reported to have health problems than their male counterparts. While 57 per cent of male elderly reported to have health problems, 65 per cent of the female elderly have reported the same. This contradictory finding calls for deeper investigation of the phenomenon.
- Health condition of an individual has something to do with his/her lifestyle. The life style of people is, to some extent, influenced by the religious faith they follow. But practice of a particular religious faith may not explain the health problems of an

individual fully. People's access to health care services, availability of quality health care providers and economic condition of the people – all these need to be taken into consideration.

- However, this trend is also consistent with facts that majority of the Jaintia elderly (51.35 per cent) reported to have health problems. Next to the Jaintias, 50 per cent of the elderly of Garo origin reported to have health problems. Least number of the Khasi elderly (38.46 per cent) reported to have health problems.

- Contrary to conventional wisdom, sample data exhibits a negative relationship between educational level and income on the one hand and health condition of the respondents on the other. It has been observed that the higher the educational and income level, the more is the health problems. One probable explanation may be that higher level of education is associated with higher level of income and higher level of income is, in turn, associated with greater profligacy. Extravagance leads to health hazards. Surprisingly, this trend is not reflected while health problems are seen against occupation. For the trend to be consistent, we would expect that higher educational achievements would lead individuals to get formal sector jobs and higher income. Hence, more formal sector employees should also report health problems. But sample data does not exhibit this pattern. In contrast, higher percentage of people engaged in farming reported to have more health problems than people engaged in formal sector (Government employees) reported. A further study is needed to look into this apparent contradiction.

- Out of 181 elderly who have specified the diseases which they suffer from, it has been observed that about 91 per cent of them suffer from age-related diseases. The old adults associated with agricultural activities suffer less than those peers associated with non-agricultural activities. Moreover, old female adults suffer less from age-related diseases than their male counterparts.
- Age-related diseases like heart problems, blood pressure, blood sugar, asthma, rheumatism, etc., are most common among the elderly. Public health policy needs to be thoroughly informed of this trend so that public health care services can focus on the health problems of the elderly. Adequate infrastructure in terms of both men and materials need to be created in public health centers in order to cater to the needs of the elderly.
- About 40 per cent of the elderly suffering from health problems has complaints about the quality of health care services provided by public health care providers.
- It has been observed that the elderly of high income group prefer health care services from the private health care providers, whereas elderly of low income group access the same from the public health care providers. As majority of the elderly

in our sample belongs to low income group, deterioration of public health care services directly impinge upon their welfare.

Trends in psychological status of the elderly

- It has been found that more number of elderly suffer from psychological adjustment problems particularly during the early years of their retirement from active life. This primarily happens due to the role erosion, as the elderly, immediately after their retirement, are stripped of the various roles and duties, both at home and workplace. It is difficult for an individual to reconcile with this change in his roles. As time passes, he gradually adjusts himself/herself with the facts of life and hence experiences lesser psychological problems. It has been found that these problems decline with the age of the elderly.

- It has been observed that the old male adults suffer more from psychological adjustment problems than their female counterparts. Probably, for the women, the role erosion is much less at old age.

- As educated and well off people can better plan and manage their old age, they face less psychological adjustment problems than those who are illiterate and poor. The percentage of people facing psychological adjustment problems declines with higher educational achievements. People with formal sector employment also exhibit less psychological adjustment problems at old age than people with informal occupations.

Trends in informal care giving to the elderly

- The matrilineal social system, which is prevalent among the Khasis, the Garos and the Jaintias in Meghalaya, vests the responsibility of care giving to the elderly with the daughter in a family. Due to this, daughters play a crucial role in providing informal care to the elderly.
- Informal care givers are the prime source of support for the elderly. Out of 231 respondents, nine have not mentioned as to with whom they are staying. As a result, our sample size in this case reduces to 222. About 97 per cent of the elderly respondents said they stay with their family members and relatives. Only two elderly stay alone. Out of 222, only four elderly were found staying at Mercy Home, a city care center. Thus, elderly in Meghalaya do not suffer much from familial and social isolation.
- It has been noted that the average family size in Meghalaya is large. On an average, an elderly is having more than five children. We find hardly any relation between the informal care giving and the number of children a person is having. That is, having more children does not guarantee higher level of informal care. Moreover, we do not find any discrimination in informal care giving to the elderly across the sex of the children – male or female.
- It has been observed that instead of number of children, the income level of children is positively

correlated with the level of informal care giving to the elderly. The level of informal care giving is interpreted in terms of the attitude of the children towards the elderly. If the needs of the elderly are attended to, it is interpreted as sympathetic attitude. It has been observed that the higher the level of income of the children, more sympathetically the elderly is treated and vice versa.

Trends in financial dependency of the elderly

- Majority of the elderly are financially dependent. This dependency rises through age. As the elderly grow older, and with no stable inflow of income, they go on drawing whatever they could amass for the old age.
- It has been observed that the elderly females are more dependent than their male counterparts. Out of 120 respondents who revealed that they are financially dependent, 62 per cent of the females and 38 per cent of the male old adults have reported financial dependency.
- It has been observed that about 80 per cent of the elderly associated with agricultural activities suffers from financial dependency. Only 39 per cent of the elderly associated with non-agricultural activities has reported financial dependency.
- Among the informal care givers, daughters play the most crucial role. In matrilineal social system, the responsibility of taking care of the elderly

members vests with the daughter in a family. About 56 per cent of the elderly in our sample fully depends on their daughter for financial support. Another 26 per cent depends on their daughters partially.

- As age progresses, more and more old adults retire from active life. This is obvious as ageing incapacitates individuals from doing physical work. Surprisingly, about 72 per cent of the elderly in the age group of 60-65 is still active. About 51 per cent of the elderly in the age group of 65-70 also remains active.

6. Recommendations and Suggestions

Old Age Security

1. It is difficult for any government to provide adequate and full proof old age security in view of the enormous cost involved in supporting a growing population of the elderly. However, the Government can provide a bare minimum financial support. It can create market and non-market instruments, and through these, encourage people to plan and save more for the old age. Government may explore various options, which will encourage people to save more during their active and working life.
2. Eligibility conditions for the old age pension need revision. Amount of pension should be considered keeping inflation and purchasing power in mind. The base amount needs upward revision.

3. The transaction cost of pension needs to be reduced.
4. Old age pension amount should be decided based on the basic need principle.
5. The delivery mechanism needs to be simplified and accessibility of the elderly needs to be improved.
6. Awareness campaign needs to be strengthened so that elderly in remote areas can avail the assistance.
7. Whatever limited old age assistance programmes are available, their distribution should focus on the self-employed, illiterate and rural elderly who are most vulnerable to old age insecurity.

Health Care Services

8. Health care services offered by both public and private health care providers need to be improved. Not that all elderly depend on public health facilities. For example, many elderly in the Jaintia Hills face less financial problem and often access private health care services. The government should encourage the private health care providers to cater medical services to the elderly at subsidized rates as part of a social commitment of the corporate entity.
9. Public health care providers need to be sensitized and made more accountable to the needs of the elderly.

10. Public health care services need to be strengthened and improved for the elderly with special units in hospitals and assured supply of medicine. It is also important to examine various models of health care so that the system can be improved.

11. Health centers exclusively for the elderly can also be considered. Health check ups and other related services need to be provided at the doorsteps to those who are immobile. Mobile medical services can go a long way in this regard.

12. Primary health centers need to be revitalized.

13. Health awareness programmes need to be organized and NGOs need to be vigorously involved in this effort.

14. Public health care institutions need to be provided with adequate infrastructure – in terms of professionals, equipments and medicines – so the elderly are better looked after.

Psychological Support

15. Informal care givers provide the psychological support to the elderly. Society needs to be sensitized about the problems of the elderly. This may be done through both formal system of education and informal socialization process. Government may launch public awareness campaigns about the need for better care of the elderly through school curriculum and also encourage community organizations and NGOs to disseminate the same.

16. Government may take initiative to introduce social service as part of school curriculum and encourage the younger generation to help and serve the elderly in surrounding areas of a school.
17. Government may declare a day for the elderly population and encourage various social institutions and civil society organizations to observe the same. Popular community leaders, officials, intellectuals and local celebrities may be involved to sensitize people on that day about care, respect and support that the elderly need.
18. On the other hand, the community too may encourage the elderly to participate in various social and community works as they are the store house of experience and knowledge. This will give them a purpose and help reduce the shocks of role erosion from which they suffer during the post-retirement life.
19. Involvement of the local community like the *Durbar Shnongs* to organize regular check up programmes may be of immense benefit.
20. As the educated elderly can better manage the retired life and suffer less from psychological adjustment problems, government may vigorously campaign for adult literacy.

Institutional and Policy Support

21. In order to achieve transparency and full implementation of the old-age pension and other schemes for the elderly, the State government may consider the following: a) create a data base

of the elderly population (village wise), identify the BPL families and enlist those elderly who are entitled to the existing two schemes, old-age pension and one-time medical grant. A village-wise household list has already been computerized by the C&RD, which is available online; b) the identified BPL elderly in each village may form an SHGs, which will ensure that the money reaches the identified beneficiaries and records/books are maintained properly; c) Another option may be the use of tiny cards, a no-frill account scheme aimed at facilitating micro-credit to poor farmers, which is being promoted by the SBI to fulfill its mandate of financial inclusion. The tiny card, just like the ATM/debit card, contains the biometric information, a digital picture of the account holder and his/her thumb impression, which authenticates the identity of the individual account holder. The same kind of no-frill accounts can be made available to the identified elderly. The government may just transfer the old-pension amount to their account, which the elderly can access through the tiny cards at their convenience. A method may be worked out to update the list of surviving elderly NOAP beneficiaries once in a year or half-yearly basis.

22. Besides, a reliable database on the health status, morbidity and disability in terms of sex, locality and socio-economic status needs to be developed.

23. An in-depth review of the existing pattern of care

for the elderly at the state, community and family levels should be initiated.

24. Institutional care like Old Age Homes and Nursing Homes for the elderly need to be promoted and strengthened.

25. As income, and not the number of children, is positively correlated with the level of elderly care, society needs to be sensitized to restrict the family size so that parents can invest more on their children. More investment on children will make them better educated. Better education will enable them to get better jobs and higher income. This will enhance the family capacity to better look after their old adults.

26. Government may consider upward revision of the retirement age of the employees, as the elderly remain active even till the mid-sixties and seventies of their life, because of advanced medicine and improved care services.

27. Finally, but not the least, media can play an important role in sensitizing the society about the problems of elderly and need for elderly care.

New Initiatives

In recent times, the society is witnessing a gradual but definite withering of joint family system. As a result, a large number of parents is not being maintained by their children as was the normal social practice. They face many problems in the absence of adequate social security. Therefore, the Ministry of Social Justice and

Empowerment has proposed law for promoting the maintenance, care and protection of older persons. The proposed legislation envisages setting up of Tribunal headed by Sub divisional magistrate in each district to deal with the maintenance claims of the parents. It has also mooted through legislation to lay down directions to the State governments/UT administrations to provide adequate medical facilities to older persons and take steps to ensure protection of their life and property.

The Ministry is also interacting with the State governments to bring about a uniformity of age for both male and female for the purpose of distribution of old age pension. Some States like Goa, Tripura and Karnataka have prepared State Policy and plan of action for the elderly people.

1

INTRODUCTION

1.1 Generalities

Ageing is a natural process that affects all human beings. Generally, it means a state of decay—a gradual deterioration of the functioning of various organs in the body and mind. It's the penultimate phase in human life before death, which is mostly marked by ill-health and associated physical and psychological problems. And because of these, ageing has serious implications on a country's economy and national security. However, advances in medical science, better nourishment and improved standards of public health have all contributed to prolonging human life. The application of science and technology, spread of medical knowledge and extension of health facilities to a wider population have brought down the birth rate and reduced the death rate especially of the elderly population.

Global scenario

The ageing of the world population is a matter of concern for everyone in all generations and in all countries. The older population is expected to quadruple over the next 50 years. This transformation in the population will change various aspects of life for individual and societies (Kapoor and Kapoor: 2004). For example, *in 1950, there were about 200 million persons aged 60 and above in the world; this figure now stands at 550 million, and is expected to reach 1 billion mark by the year 2020. Even more dramatic is the expected increase in the number of very old people (aged 80+ years); that group is projected to grow by a factor of 8 to 10 times... between 1950 and 2025* (Atal : 2001). In the same way, many studies have indicated the growth of elderly population. A view of this growing literature is presented in the succeeding paragraphs.

According to a study by Desjarlais et al (1999), the population of the elderly in the world has been growing rapidly from the middle of the 20th century. It projected that *the number of aged in the world population will be more than double from 500 million in 1990 to over one billion by 2025.* The rapid increase in the population of the elderly in the world has caught the attention and concern of the United Nations and in its *World Population Prospect, Estimates and Projections*, the aged/elderly population (over 60 years of age) was estimated at 5.3 percent in 1980 and is expected to jump to 7.7 percent in the year 2000 and 13.3 percent by the year 2025. According to the United Nations (1988), the most dominant trend from the mid-Eighties to the middle of the 21st century is likely to be the ageing of the population in the developed as well as the developing world. The number of the elderly may increase to one billion by the year 2030 and about 50 percent of these would be from Asia, with major contributions from India and China (Thakur: 2002).

The rise in the population of the elderly was thought to be a concern only of the developed countries but it has now become an equally important issue even in the developing countries as well. One of the reasons why the social scientists from the developing countries did not show much interest in the problem of ageing is that the proportion of the old age people is comparatively small and the longevity is still shorter in the developing countries compared to the developed world. Unlike the West where the nuclear families and individualization of personalities are the norm, it is quite natural that the developed world has taken the lead in raising the debate regarding the problem of the elderly. In 1990, the developing countries had only 6.9 percent of the population, which is 60 years and above as compared to 17.1 percent in the developed nations. However, changes are taking place the other way round. It has been projected that compared to the 1990 figures, the developing countries like India, China and Mexico will witness 200-280 per cent increase in the population of the elderly by 2025, while in the developed nations, there will be only an increase of 33.65 percent (Legare: 1993).

The developed countries are in a position to meet the challenges but the developing countries are facing a resource crunch on the one hand and rising unemployment, urban migration and population overgrowth etc. on the other. Hence, it is not going to be an easy task to provide proper health care services and fulfill other needs of the growing number of elderly, unless strategies and approaches are evolved that are cost effective and sustainable.

The United Nations Principles for Older Persons were evolved in recognition of the fact that *in all countries, individuals are reaching an advanced age in greater numbers and in better health than ever before.* They emphasized the need *for a variety of policy responses because of tremendous diversity in the situation of older persons not only between countries but within countries, and between individuals.* They also recommended that "*opportunities must be provided for willing and capable older persons to participate in, and contribute to the ongoing activities of society*". The 18 principles enunciated by the United Nations fall into five clusters, namely, independence, participation, care, self-fulfillment, and dignity (Modi: 2001)

Recognizing the importance of this particular age group, in 1990, the UN General Assembly designated October 1 as the *International Day of Older Persons* for celebrating and acknowledging the contribution of older people to society. The United Nations Principles for Older Persons, adopted in 1991, are best summed up in the logo: *To add life to the years that have been added to life.* A conceptual framework for International Year of Older Person (IYOP), which is based on the International Plan of Action on Ageing (1982) and the Principles for Older Persons (1991), was formulated and submitted by the Secretary General to the 50th session of the General Assembly in 1995. The 1997 Operational Framework also assisted in setting the scene for the International Year of Older Persons, 1999. The overall theme for IYOP was *Towards a Society for All Ages,* which reflects a growing concern for ensuring age-integration and multi-generational relationship (Modi: 2001).

Since the time the United Nations dedicated the year 1999 to the aged/elderly as the International Year for Older Persons, a large number of literature has flooded the global print market focusing on a wide range of issues and concerns related to the elderly population of the world. India for its part has not been lagging behind in its approach to its elderly.

National scenario: India

As has been reflected earlier, India being a developing country with a large population, one of the many challenges facing the country is the growth of elderly population, which is growing much faster than the overall global population. Again with improved health care facilities and standards of living, life expectancy of Indians is going up. Elderly population has attracted the attention of health planners, economists and demographers alike as there has been a steep rise in the world population of people aged 60 years and above in the last five decades. Demographers are predicting a steeper rise in the coming years. Indian population is heading towards in what may be termed as the 'explosion of the aged/elderly'.

Many studies have indicated the rise in population of the elderly population in India. According to the Research, Reference and Training Division, Ministry of Information and Broadcasting, Government of India, *the population of older persons 60+ in India ranks fourth highest in the world and by the end of the present century it will be second only to China. Today, India is home to one out of every ten senior citizens of the world* (Research, Reference and Training Division, Ministry of Information and Broadcasting, 2001). According to the Indian census figures, the proportion of elderly persons in India has risen from 5.63 per cent in 1961 to 6.58 per cent in 1991, to around 7.08 percent in 2001 and will be somewhere 9.87 percent in 2021 (Yadav: 2004). Similarly, Sundari and Geetha (1999) also projected that the population of the aged will rise *from 25.6 millions in 1961, the number of those over 60 years is expected to reach 340 million in 2061.* The United Nations too declared that India would become an ageing society where the aged would account for more than seven percent of the total population of the world (Uplaonkar: 1999). At present the estimated number of persons aged 60 and above is about 70 million which is likely to touch 177 million by 2025, about 25 percent of whom would be above 80years of age (Thakur: 2002).

From figure 1.1, we find that the elderly population was 12 million in 1901, 19 million in 1951, 77 million in 2001 and is expected to go up to 177 million in 2025.

Growing population of the Elderly

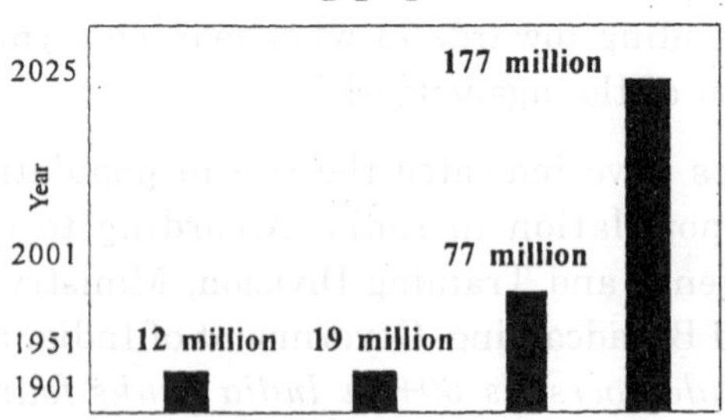

Year	No of Older Persons
1901	12 million
1951	19 million
2001	77 million.
2025	177 million
(projected)	

Source: www.helpageindia.org

Figure 1.1

Thus the population of 60+ is assuming an enormous size and the tremendous growth of the population of the elderly and its growing proportion in the total population are creating new problems for the society and for themselves (Singh: 2001).

Recognizing this, the Constitution of India in its Directive Principles recognizes the need for the care of the elderly. Art 41, section 125 of the Criminal Procedure, 1973 and section 20(3) of the Hindu Adaptation and Maintenance are a few legislative measures for the security of its aged/elderly. India's Eight Five-Year Plan also encourages voluntary or non-governmental organizations for providing old age homes, day-care centers, mobile medical units and other programmes (Sundari and Geetha: 1999).

The Ministry of Social Justice and Empowerment (MSJE) has been implementing a Central scheme of assistance for the programmes relating to the aged/elderly from November 1992. This is indicated in the *National Policy on Older Persons*, MSJE, Government of India (attached in the annexure). Meghalaya, too, is said to be following this policy in relation to the elderly persons in the State. Under the central scheme, financial assistance is provided to voluntary organizations for establishing and maintaining of day-care centers, old-age homes, mobile medicare units as well as for supporting and strengthening non-institutional services for the elderly/aged. This scheme, revised in 1998-99, is called 'An Integrated Programme for Older Persons'. Under the revised scheme, up to 90 percent of the cost of the project will be provided by the Government of

India and the remaining shall be borne by the organization or institution concerned (Research, Reference & Training Division :2001).

1.1.1 Elderly: Meaning of the term

Who are the aged/elderly? There is no single accepted definition of the elderly, which is unanimously accepted worldwide. The terms elderly, aged and senior citizen have been used interchangeably. They all imply the same meaning of old age (Modi:1997). Different scholars have different views and opinions on the elderly. The concept of old age is not the same throughout the world. There are three different cut off age for elderly-55 years, 60 years and 65 years (Sahu: 1998). For example, when a 15 year old boy considers a 30 year old man elderly, the latter treats a 50 year old man elderly and so on so forth. So, there is no clear cut definition as to whom we can consider elderly/aged. Therefore chronological age is not a satisfactory criterion for determining old age because there are individual variations in the rate of physiological ageing. In a sense the old are those people whom the society categorizes as old (Mohanty: 2004).

The Collin's Dictionary of Sociology says that *it is the last part of the individual's life course, associated with declining faculties, low social worth and detachment from previous social commitments. It is a social construct rather than a biological stage, since its onset signifies very historically and culturally* (Mohanty: 2004). In the opinion of Soodan (1975), *the beginning of old age in an individual is associated with different conditions or changes occurring in one's life, viz., the onset of the graying of the hair, the advent of bifocals, a serious impairment of vital physical components, failure of the individual to function independently, ceasing to be productive and imposition of an arbitrary retirement age by the society*. Old age is generally associated with fatigue, decline in functional capacity of the organs of the body, decrease ability to cope with the stress of disease or trauma.

While advancing old age, disabilities that impair daily living activities are very common in old age. It also refers to the age in which most people retire from work and claim for benefits such as pensions. According to Shankar (1992), old age *is often a time of loss in terms of relationships. Retirement from active work means loss of contact with co-workers. Old age may also mean that old people staying back in their villages and towns while their children move away from homes, and relatives and friends are lost through death or distance.* In other words, old age may be termed as the later part of life of an individual in which symptoms of physical deterioration begins to appear. It indicates the manifestation of physiological, social and psychological changes.

However, the point at which old age begins cannot be specified. For administrative purposes, such as determining retirement age, an arbitrary chronological age is used which has no relationship to physiological age or to function/working capacity. But a widely used dividing line is retirement. Retirement age in most countries is fixed between 55 and 65 years. This varies from country to country and the level of development of that particular country. The United Nations defines elderly citizens as those who are over 65 years old because there is often obvious deterioration in their health condition. Most of the Western countries have set the age of 65 as the year of retirement. Old age is usually regarded as synonymous with retirement age. In India, the age of retirement varies from 55-65. The Indian census has adopted the age of 60 for classifying a person as old. Thus in this study, 60 years and over is taken as the elderly population.

1.1.2 Problems of the Elderly

The problems of the senior citizens in India and for that matter in most of the third world countries are different from the problems of the old persons in the developed and western countries. The social institutions, cultural milieu, customs, traditions, religion, community control and individual as well as group psychology of the two worlds are quite different. In India, whenever the problems of the elderly are discussed from academic or policy orientation point of view it is by and large the middle class and other elite whose problems get highlightened. However, there is hardly any concerted effort to measure the problems of the elderly in the poorer sections of the society. It is, therefore, imperative to mention here that in a society where more than 70 per cent population lives in the villages and an aggregate of more than 50 per cent of the urban and rural population live below the poverty line, it is not only the problem of the elderly that is important but it is the problem of poverty which also needs adequate attention (Suguna: 2004).

Old age is generally accompanied by a number of problems that the elderly have to face and adjust with in varying degrees. Loss of economic independence and physical vigour and the emergence of various types of degenerative diseases change an elderly from an independent, self-supporting individual to one who needs help from his children, members of the family and the society in general. Absence of common interests and lack of extensive and regular interaction with the younger members in the family may result in social isolation and loneliness of the elderly.

The obligation of the Indian family system to look after the elderly continues to be discharged even today. There are, however, some emerging stresses and strains of the forces of urbanization, industrialization and modernization which have given rise to change in social and family structure resulting in declining role and status of the elderly in the society. The spread of education and greater social mobility have resulted in the out migration of children from their native homes in search of jobs, leaving the elderly with none to look after them. In this changing situation, the old persons feel depressed and deprived. A sense of insecurity and helplessness prevails. Moreover, the loss of their status in the family and the community becomes a source of utter frustration and maladjustment. Today, it is evidently pronounced that young people are independent and they often choose the lifestyle of the western societies. Thus the image of the elderly then reflects powerlessness. They are the least noticed of the destitute.

In India studies show that the family is the prime source of social, economic and emotional support in physical care. It has been observed that the care of the elderly depends upon the status and prestige enjoyed by them in the family. This status depends on several factors, viz., the material possession and physical disability to share the family burden. This status, in turn, becomes the factor which decides one's well being and care in the family. Any dereliction in the duty of the elderly will axe the harmonious relation in the family with other members in no time. Well being of the elderly depends on the nature and extent of factors such as role erosion, role overload, role isolation, role expectation and role conflict (Bali: 1999). Let's briefly run over these factors.

Role Erosion

An elderly in his active life assumes various roles and social position and plays those roles according to his/her ability and capacity. As the ageing sets in, s/he is stripped of his/her various roles and duties, thus, leading to the role erosion. The erosion is combined with the change in the social structure and relationship of the elderly in the family. Similarly, one may find substantial change in work relationship and economic transition in cases of role erosion. This causes many a time a great deal of dependency of the older person.

Role Overload

It leads to stress, strain and fatigue, both physically, psychologically, economically as well as socially for the elderly. Such type of role overload is seen particularly in cases of women. The elderly women are bound by various domestic changes and other economic activities in her youth and supplementing the family income in their middle age. She takes care of the young and old members of the family to the best of her capacity. Due to the onset of age and other physical vagaries, it becomes too demanding for her to comply with all sorts of expectations by the younger family members. This also sometimes has deleterious effects on their mental and physical health, caused due to role overload.

Role Isolation

Role Isolation occurs when an individual, particularly an elderly feels that s/he is kept out of whatever happening in the family. Being replaced, sidelined from their earlier position of importance, could have serious consequences on the well being of the elderly. This could lead to loneliness and boredom. Perceived non-usefulness causes a lot of unhappiness. This problem is found much severe among widows, separated or divorced or in cases of desertion.

Role Expectation

Every individual in a family has certain ascribed role by virtue of being born or being part of a particular family, so they play a set of defined roles. At times role player subjects himself to an evaluation in keeping with his or her own expectations of the role being played. In the event of conflict normal role play of the elderly will be adversely affected and it will lead to distortion and deviation in routine expectation. This could arise when the elderly expects a certain kind of help or care but is not forthcoming. Such situation can affect the elderly deleteriously.

Role Conflict

Role conflict could arise between the elderly and others, primarily due to differences in the perceptions and the values attached to the performance of the roles. Recognition of this indicates the fact that conflicting needs and desires of the elderly and others cannot possibly be fulfilled due to various limitations within the family or outside. Besides these, factors like personal inadequacies, i.e., physical, economic and social and resource inadequacy also impinge upon the well being of the elderly.

1.2 Objectives of the Study

The broad objective of the study is to understand the nature and magnitude of the problem of the elderly persons in Meghalaya. This broad objective entails in the following specific points:

- to study the growth in population of the elderly persons
- to study the status of living arrangements, family life and inter-generational adjustment of the elderly
- to examine the social and economic status of the elderly
- to probe into their general health condition and access to health care services
- to study the recommendations of the society and the elderly towards the elderly welfare
- to make suggestions for implementation

1.3 Methodology

The study was conducted in the seven district headquarters of Meghalaya - Shillong (East Khasi Hills), Nongstoin (West Khasi Hills), Nongpoh (Ri-Bhoi), Williamnagar (East Garo Hills), Tura (West Garo Hills), Baghmara (South Garo Hills) and Jowai (Jaintia Hills). In total 231 elderly persons were selected using a simple random sampling technique. The respondents comprise of both male and female population of 60 years and above. The data was collected through a structured questionnaire (enclosed in the annexure) which covered different aspects related to general information (profile of the elderly), health, socio-economic status and the recommendations on the elderly. The Data collection and report writing were carried out during June-November 2005.

In course of the study, an extensive literature review was conducted. All the available and relevant secondary sources of information both published and unpublished were collected, reviewed and analyzed. The other relevant supplementary information were also collected from available secondary sources like census reports, Government reports etc.

Interviews were also taken from Key Informants (KIs) during the field work after informing them about the proposed project. The list of KIs included key officials from the State Government, headmen, community/social worker, NGOs etc. from each district in order to get information about the status, problems and welfare of the elderly population in the region.

Before the start of the fieldwork, the field team investigators were given an orientation of the principles of research ethics and a pilot survey was carried on the same day in order to test the effectiveness of the questionnaire. In doing so whatever problems they faced were discussed and alternatives were planned in order to get the desired data as per the questionnaire.

Data Collection

Every selected elderly person was personally contacted when he/she was relatively free. The purpose of investigation was explained and their co-operation sought. Good rapport was established with them through periodic visits to their households. The co-operation of the family members was also sought in eliciting information from the elderly. The elderly were encouraged to express their opinions freely and frankly. As far as possible, the information was collected from the respondents when they were alone to avoid any complications. To elicit correct information, thorough probing was done wherever necessary.

Data for the study was collected through :

1. personal interview with the respondents with the help of an interview schedule
2. informal interviews with the various key informants including the family and friends of the elderly
3. published and unpublished material regarding issues pertaining to the elderly

A simple statistical method has been used to present and analyze the quantifiable responses. The data was presented in simple tables, which had been particularly useful in the analysis of respondent's attitudes, opinions and behavioural orientations concerning the self in different life situations.

2

STATE PROFILE

Meghalaya, the 21st State of the Indian Union was created under the Assam Re-organisation (Meghalaya) Act, 1969 of Parliament passed on December 24, 1969. It was inaugurated by the then Prime Minister, Mrs Indira Gandhi in April 21, 1970 as an autonomous State. Till 1971, Meghalaya was a part of Assam. It was made a full-fledged State on January 21, 1972. It shares international boundaries with Bangladesh on the West and South, and with Assam on the North and East. There are seven districts in the State – East Khasi Hills, West Khasi Hills, South Garo Hills, West Garo Hills, East Garo Hills, Jaintia Hills and Ribhoi covering an area of 22,489 sq. km with a population density of 103 per sq. km. These districts are divided into subdivisions and Blocks for administrative purposes.

The whole of Meghalaya is a plateau, which is known as the Meghalaya Plateau or Shillong Plateau. The main urban centres of Meghalaya are Shillong, Tura and Jowai. These towns have developed mainly due to their administrative functions. A number of market centres with several urban characteristics are growing along the main roads.

As per the 2001 provisional census report, the total population of Meghalaya is 23,06,069 with 975 females per 1000 males. Meghalaya's population predominantly belongs to the scheduled tribe communities. The main tribes in Meghalaya are the Khasis, the Jaintias and the Garos. The Khasis and the Jaintias are Proto-Austroloid Monkhmer race and the Garos belong to Tibeto-Burman race. These tribes are matrilineal in inheritance, descent and residence. The main languages spoken in the state are: Khasi, Jaintia, Garo and English. Christianity is the principal religion in the State. The other religious followers such as Animism, Hinduism, Muslims, Buddhists and Sikhs constitute a minority.

Meghalaya has abundant but untapped natural resources, including coal, limestone, quartz, mica, gypsum, bauxite, and other minerals. Rice, maize and wheat are the main crops. Citrus, pineapple, bananas, peas and plums are grown in large areas. Main cash crops are potatoes, jute, cotton, mustard, areca nut, ginger, turmeric, and black pepper. The State does not have large-scale industries; there are a few small-scale industrial firms. The British rule brought in great socio-economic and religious change in the lives of the local people. There are no railways in Meghalaya. The national highways run through the State. The only airport in the state is located at Umroi, 31 km from Shillong.

Shillong

Shillong (Latitude 25° 35' North and Longitude 91°5'E) is the capital of Meghalaya and the Headquarter of the North-Eastern Council and the Eastern Command of the Indian Air-Force. It is about 103 km to the South of Guwahati and is located at an altitude of 1500 meters above mean sea level.

Shillong has cosmopolitan culture with many tribal and non-tribal populations from other states living in peace and harmony. The ideal climate with pleasant summer accounts for its charm as a hill station. It is a place of attraction for the tourists. Since its establishment in 1864, development in various aspects has grown considerably. Shillong has developed as a major educational centre in the region, with a renowned university, large number of schools and colleges. The major attraction apart from the educational centres is its industrial, commercial and administrative growth in the last few years. The migrant population at present consists of a significant sub-population in the State. A sizeable population of the Nagas, the Mizos, the Manipuris, the Bodos, the Arunachalis, the Tripuris, the Assamese, the Biharis, the Bengalis, and the Nepalese also lives in the State. The mode of transportation for commodities and goods is mainly through the National Highways.

Tura

Tura (latitude 25° 32' North and longitude 90° 14' East) is about 323 km from Shillong. It is the district headquarters of the West Garo hills. The highest peak of this range is the Nokrek (1412 metres) which lies 13km south-east Tura. It is one of the most developed towns of the Garo hills. It has developed due to its administrative functions. The other functions of this town include trade and commerce, transport services etc. and most transactions are done here. There are a number of schools and colleges and many people from all over the Garo hills come to this town to pursue their studies. The standard of living is higher at Tura than any other parts of the Garo Hills district. The important road link is the Shillong-Nongstoin-Tura Road.

Williamnagar

Williamnagar is the district headquarters of the East Garo Hills. It is situated on the banks of river Simsang and is navigable for a distance of about 30 km. The district was named after the first Chief Minister of Meghalaya, Captain Williamson Sangma. This small town has quite a number of localities with government offices, a small market and a few schools and colleges. The people of this town are far backward than Tura. Almost 60 per cent of the inhabitants of this town is poor.

Baghmara

It is about 110 km from Tura and the district headquarters of the South Garo Hills. This town is also situated on the bank of river Simsang and shares an international border with Bangladesh. The people of this town are far backward than Tura or Williamnagar. It has a small market, one college and few schools. Many people come from poor families. The important road links are Damdara- Davigiri- Nangalbibra- Baghmara

Road and Paikan- Bajengdoba- Tura- Dalu- Baghmara Road

Jowai

Jowai is situated 64 km away from Shillong. It is the district headquarters of the Jaintia Hills. It is situated in 25°26' North latitude and 92°12' East longitude above the sea level. It is bounded on the North and East by the State of Assam and on the South by Bangladesh and on the West by the Khasi Hills District. The other functions of this town include trade and commerce, transport services, administrative functions etc.

Nongpoh

Nongpoh is the Headquarter of the Ri Bhoi District. It is situated at a distance of 54 kms from Shillong on the Shillong-Guwahati Road. Being an administrative centre, it houses a number of Government offices. Nongpoh has served as a halting station for travelers ever since the opening of the road linking Shillong with Guwahati in the last century. It has developed into a small market place where vegetables and fruits grown locally are sold.

Nongstoin

It is the headquarters of the West Khasi Hills district. Nongstoin is situated at a distance of 96kms from Shillong. The literacy rate is around 52 per cent and the population is around two lakhs. This district is famous for its knowledge of local medicine, which attracts a lot of visitors from all over the State. Nongstoin lies on the route leading westwards to the Garo Hills and Northwards to Mawthengkut and other places. The road between Mairang and Nongstoin passes through some of the most beautiful spots in the hills, part of which runs along the Kynshi river.

2.1 Current scenario of Elderly persons in Meghalaya

Among the traditional tribal societies of Meghalaya where the family and kinship ties are still strong, the elderly are not treated as a problem. The elderly also do not find it difficult to spend their last days since their family and kin groups need their advice and guidance. The elderly could disengage them from life to any extent, and yet retain their position of respect. An attitude of reverence towards the aged/elderly is considered a virtue and nothing important could take place in the family without the sanction and blessings of the old. The elderly have been assigned a place of honour and respect and are well integrated in the society. The responsibility of looking after old people is taken for granted. So the elderly too never consider themselves useless and also do not find it a problem to spend the remaining part of their life in the company of their kith and kin with dignity.

This scenario is, however, gradually changing with deepening the forces of modernization. Traditional values are giving way to predicaments of modern living. The informal care taking system built-in traditional social and family structures is slowly fading away. The change in social family structures is resulting in declining role and status of the elderly in the society. In this changing situation the old persons feel depressed, insecure and deprived in their family and community.

Many of them are trapped in misery through a combination of low income, poor health and lack of care. Furthermore, the traditional support structure of the family is increasingly unable to cope with the problems. With more and more children unable to take care of their parents and with the gradual increase of the elderly population, there is a growing population of destitute elderly in the age group of 60 plus. This indicates that matters will worsen in the years to come.

In 1991, Meghalaya had a population of 1,774,778 with 51.14 percent male and 48.58 percent female. The elderly constituted 4.5 per cent of the total population. Their absolute number was 78,742. Of the total elderly, 55.1 per cent was male and 44.9 per cent was female. While in the rural areas the proportion of the elderly male was higher than the female elderly, in the urban areas their proportion was almost the same.

The Table 2.2.1 presents a total of 1,677,707 in the age-group of 0-59 that constitute 94.53 per cent of the elderly population. The male and female percentage includes 50.95 and 49.04 respectively. The persons whose age is not stated are also indicated here. Further, this table shows the number of elderly population of 60+ in Meghalaya in 1991. In 1991, of the overall total population (1,774,778) there is 1.84 per cent elderly in the age of 60-64, 1.00 per cent in the age of 65-69, 0.77 per cent in the age of 70-74. In the age group of 75-79, there is 0.37 per cent elderly and 0.45 per cent elderly belong to the age group of 80 years and above. Out of the total of each age group, the elderly male population includes 55.97 per cent for 60-64 years, 55.13 per cent for 65-69 years, 54.37 per cent for 70-74 years, 54.04 per cent for 75-79 years and 53.43 per cent for 80 years and above. Similarly, the female elderly belonging to the age group of 60-64 is 44.09 per cent, 65-69 years is 44.86 per cent, 70-74 years is 45.63 per cent, 75-79 years is 45.96 per cent and 46.56 per cent for 80 years and above.

Table 2.2.1
Elderly population 60+ in Meghalaya 1991

Age group	*Total*	*% of total age group*	*Male*	*4 as 2 % of*	*Female*	*6 as % of 2*
1	2	3	4	5	6	7
0-59	1677707	94.53	854848	50.95	822859	49.04
60-64	32,654	1.84	18,277	55.97	14,377	44.09
65-69	17,803	1.00	9,816	55.13	7,987	44.86
70-74	13,685	0.77	7,440	54.37	6,245	45.63
75-79	6,508	0.37	3,517	54.04	2,991	45.96
80+	8092	0.45	4,324	53.43	3,768	46.56
Total (60-80 & above)	78742	4.43	43374	55.08	35368	44.92
Age not stated	18329	1.03	9465	51.64	8864	48.36
All age group	1774778	100.0	907687	51.14	867091	48.85

Source: Census of India: 1991

In 2001, while the population of Meghalaya has gone up to 2,318,822, with 50.72 percent male and 49.28 percent female. The total number of the elderly was

1,05,726. Of the total elderly, 51.09 per cent was male and 48.91 per cent was female (Table 2.2.2). A comparison between the 1991 and 2001 population census reveals that while the decadal growth rate of population in Meghalaya has been 30.65 per cent, the same for elderly population stands at 34.27 per cent. This clearly indicates that elderly population in Meghalaya is growing at a faster rate than the decadal growth rate of the overall population. Thus, as far as the change in age-composition of population is concerned, Meghalaya exhibits a similar trend as has been observed elsewhere. Therefore, public authorities in Meghalaya have reasons to be concerned about the problems of the elderly. This trend calls for appropriate public interventions in order to ensure the welfare of the elderly in the State.

Furthermore, Table 2.2.2 presents the total of 2,209,936 for the age-group of 0-59 which comprise of 95.30 percent. The male and the female percentage includes 50.69 and 49.31 respectively. The persons whose age is not stated are also indicated here. This table also shows the number of the elderly population of 60+ in Meghalaya in 2001. In 2001, of the overall total population, there is 1.69 per cent elderly in the age of 60-64, 1.15 per cent in the age of 65-69, 0.81 per cent in the age of 70-74. In the age group of 75-79, there is 0.42 per cent elderly and 0.48 per cent elderly belongs to the age group of 80 years and above. Out of the total of each age group, the elderly male population of the total of each age group includes 51.97 per cent for 60-64 years, 51.05 per cent for 65-69 years, 50.67 per cent for 70-74 years, 51.03 per cent for 75-79 years and 48.48 per cent for 80 years and above. Similarly, the female elderly belonging to the age group of 60-64 is 48.00 per cent, 65-69 years is 48.95 per cent, 70-74 years is 49.33 per cent, 75-79 years is 48.97 per cent and the female elderly who have attained the age of 80 years and above constitute 51.22 per cent.

Table 2.2.2
Elderly population 60+ in Meghalaya (2001)

Age group	*Total*	*% of total age group*	*Male*	*4 as 2 % of*	*Female*	*6 as % of 2*
1	2	3	4	5	6	7
0-59	2209936	95.30	1120270	50.69	1089666	49.31
60-64	39,326	1.69	20,448	51.97	18,878	48.00
65-69	26,664	1.15	13,611	51.05	13,053	48.95
70-74	18,797	0.81	9,525	50.67	9,272	49.33
75-79	9,696	0.42	4,948	51.03	4,748	48.97
80+	11,243	0.48	5,484	48.78	5,759	51.22
Total (60-80 & above)	1,05,726	4.56	54,016	51.09	51,710	48.91
Age not stated	3160	0.14	1801	56.99	1359	43.00
All age group	2318822	100.00	1176087	50.72	1142735	49.28

Source: Census of India: 2001

The growth of the elderly population in Meghalaya is indicated in figure 2.2.1. The age group of 60-64 shows a growth rate of four per cent, the age-group of 65-69 exhibits a growth rate of 30 per cent and 70-74 exhibits a growth of 18 per cent. The growth rate of the age-group of 75-79 is 29 per cent and for the 80 above age-group, the growth rate is 19 per cent.

Total growth rate (in percentage) of Elderly Population 60+in Meghalaya (1991-2001)

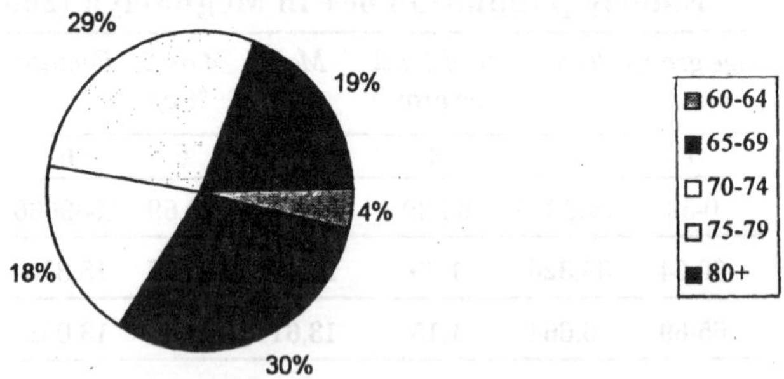

Source: Census of India

Figure 2.2.1

The growth rate of the male and the female elderly population is shown in figure 2.2.2. The age group of 60-64 shows a decline in growth rate of the male (-4.8 per cent) but an increase of the female (14.5 per cent). In the age group of 65-69, there is an increase of 18.3 per cent of the male and 41.4 per cent of the female. In the age-group of 70-74, growth rate of the male is 9.3 per cent and 27.5 per cent of the female. In the 75-79 age group, the growth rate of the male is 19.2 per cent and 36.7 per cent of the female, and among the elderly above 80 years, the growth rate of the male is 6.7 per cent and 30.9 per cent of the female.

Growth rate of male and female Elderly Population in Meghalaya (1991-2001)

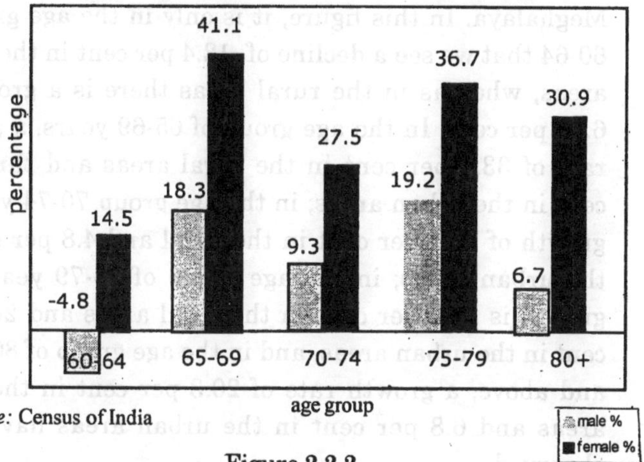

Source: Census of India

Figure 2.2.2

Growth rate of Elderly Population by rural and urban areas of Meghalaya (1991-2001)

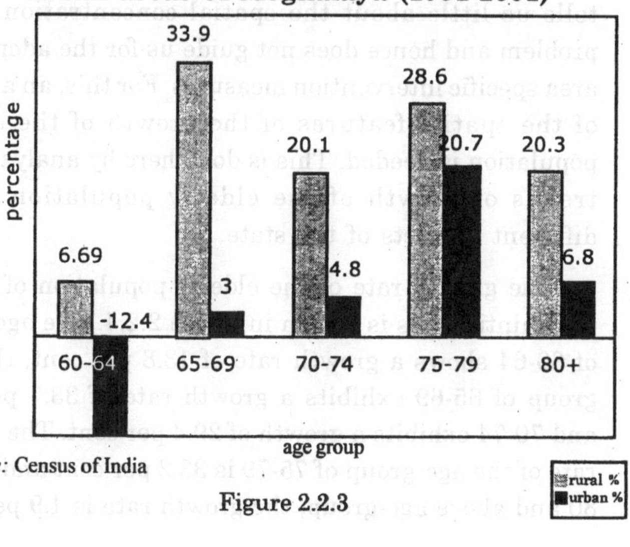

Source: Census of India

Figure 2.2.3

Figure 2.2.3 shows the growth rate of the elderly population in the rural and the urban areas of Meghalaya. In this figure, it is only in the age group of 60-64 that we see a decline of -12.4 per cent in the urban areas, whereas in the rural areas there is a growth of 6.69 per cent. In the age group of 65-69 years, a growth rate of 33.9 per cent in the rural areas and three per cent in the urban areas; in the age group 70-74 years, a growth of 20.1 per cent in the rural and 4.8 per cent in the urban areas; in the age group of 75-79 years, the growth is 28.6 per cent in the rural areas and 20.7 per cent in the urban areas, and in the age group of 80 years and above, a growth rate of 20.3 per cent in the rural areas and 6.8 per cent in the urban areas have been observed.

However, the growth scenario of the elderly population in Meghalaya, as has been portrayed so far, tells us little about the spatial concentration of the problem and hence does not guide us for the adoption of area specific intervention measures. For this, an analysis of the spatial features of the growth of the elderly population is needed. This is done here by analyzing the trends of growth of the elderly population in the different districts of the state.

The growth rate of the elderly population of 60+ in the Jaintia Hills is shown in figure 2.2.4. The age group of 60-64 shows a growth rate of 13.8 per cent, the age-group of 65-69 exhibits a growth rate of 33.7 per cent and 70-74 exhibits a growth of 29.4 per cent. The growth rate of the age-group of 75-79 is 33.2 per cent and for the 80 and above age-group, the growth rate is 4.9 per cent.

Growth rate of Elderly Population (60+) in Jaintia Hills (1991-2001)

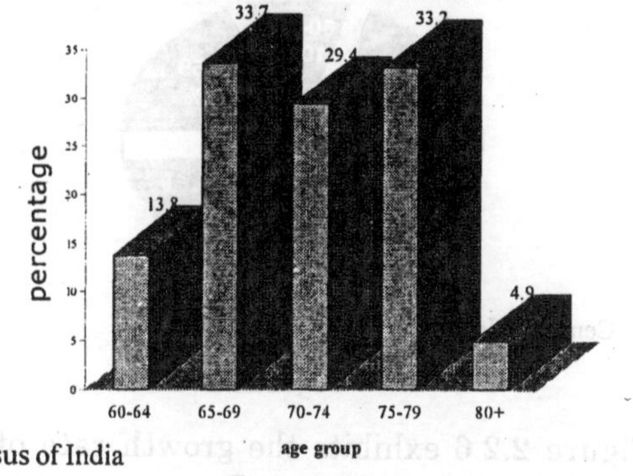

Source: census of India

Figure 2.2.4

In the East Khasi Hills, however, there is a decline in the growth rate. As observed in figure 2.2.5, the age group of 60-64 indicates a decline of -28.4 per cent, 65-69 exhibits a decline of -14.6 per cent, 70-74 years registers a decline of -15.9 per cent, 75-79 years shows a decline of -6.9 per cent and 80 years and above exhibits a decline of -9.6 per cent.

Growth rate of Elderly Population (60+) in East Khasi Hills (1991-2001)

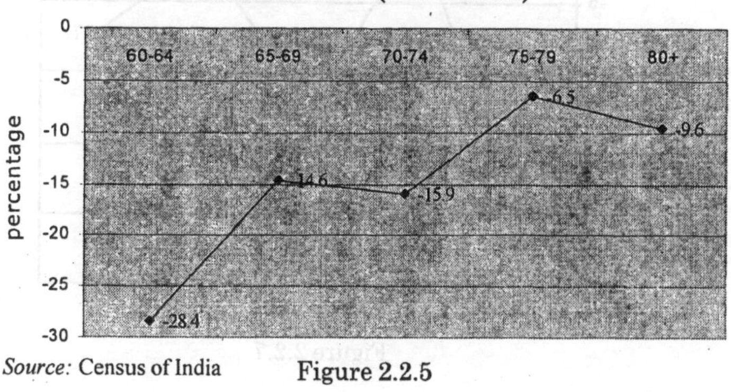

Source: Census of India

Figure 2.2.5

Growth rate of Elderly Population (60+) in West Khasi Hills (1991-2001)

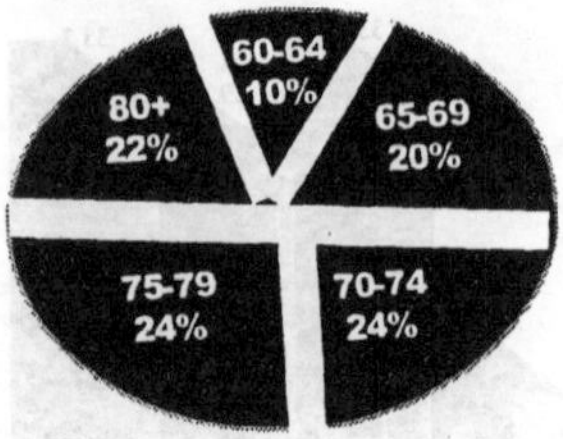

Source: Census of India

Figure 2.2.6

Figure 2.2.6 exhibits the growth rate of the elderly in the West Khasi Hills. The age group of 60-64 shows a growth rate of 10 per cent, the age-group of 65-69 exhibits a growth rate of 20 per cent and 70-74 exhibits a growth of 24 per cent. The growth rate of the age-group of 75-79 is 24 per cent and in the 80 and above age-group, the growth rate is 22 per cent.

Growth rate of Elderly Population (60+) in West Garo Hills (1991-2001)

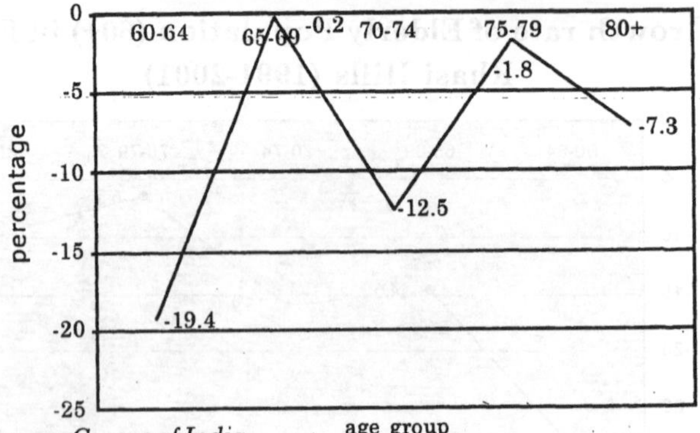

Source: Census of India

Figure 2.2.7

Like the East Khasi Hills, the West Garo Hills too shows a decline in the growth rate of the elderly population during 1991-2001. As observed in figure 2.2.7, the age group of 60-64 indicates a decline of -19.4 per cent, 65-69 shows a decline of -0.2 per cent, 70-74 years exhibits a decline of -12.5 per cent, 75-79 years shows a decline of -1.8 per cent and 80 years and above exhibits a decline of -7.3 per cent.

Figure 2.2.8 indicates the growth rate of the elderly population (60+) in East Garo Hills during 1991-2001. The age group of 60-64 shows a growth rate of 14 per cent, the age-group of 65-69 exhibits a growth rate of 33 per cent and 70-74 exhibits a growth of 17 per cent. The growth rate of the age-group of 75-79 is 22 per cent and the 80 and above age-group, the growth rate is 14 per cent.

Growth rate of Elderly Population (60+) in West Garo Hills (1991-2001)

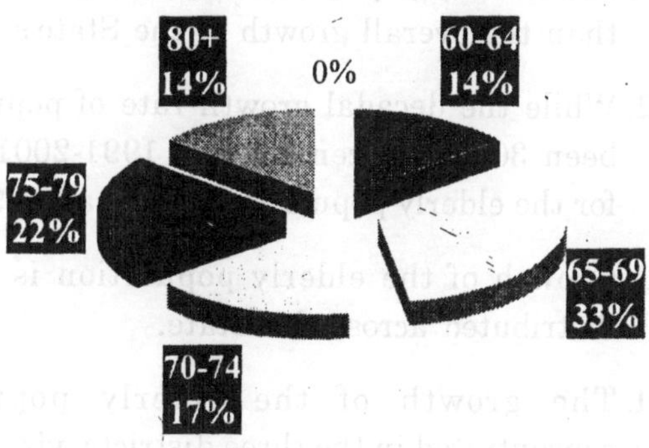

Source: Census of India

Fig 2.2.8

Spatial distribution of the growth rate of the elderly population shows that the growth is not evenly distributed across the State. Rather, the growth rate of the elderly population is concentrated in the three districts, viz., the Jaintia Hills, the West Khasi Hills and the East Garo Hills. All these three districts being predominantly rural, it is, thus evident that rural Meghalaya bears much of the burden of the elderly population. Public intervention measures, thus, need to have a rural focus. Special measures need to be designed for and implemented in areas where the elderly population is concentrated.

Conclusion : Trends and Areas of Concern

The growth of the elderly population in Meghalaya exhibits the following trends which need to be noted by the society in general and the public authority in particular for devising adequate intervention measures.

1. The Elderly population is growing at a faster rate than the overall growth of the State's population.
2. While the decadal growth rate of population has been 30.65 per cent during 1991-2001, the same for the elderly population stands at 34.97 per cent.
3. Growth of the elderly population is not evenly distributed across the State.
4. The growth of the elderly population is concentrated in the three districts, viz., the Jaintia Hills, the West Khasi Hills and the East Garo Hills.

5. Rural Meghalaya bears much of the burden of the elderly population than its urban counterparts.
6. While in 1991, longevity of the females at age 60 was higher than the males, this gap has reduced in 2001.

3

GENERAL INFORMATION AND STATUS OF THE ELDERLY

A study of the general information of the elderly involves an analysis of their age, gender, marital status, religion, community, educational levels and other attributes. The elderly population as shown by this study covers a diverse group who differ from each other in a variety of ways. There are those just turned 60 who are keen on earning a living and supporting themselves and their families as long as possible. There are Christians, Hindus, Muslims etc., there are single and married people, well-to-do as well as penniless individuals depending upon others for their essential needs. There are people who are healthy and unhealthy, literate and illiterate and so on. These characteristics of the elderly are discussed below.

Any meaningful study of the elderly population must take into account the general background in order to get a brief idea, which describes the physical as well as the socio-psychological well being of the elderly. These influence the quality of life of the older age group (60 plus years) much more than that of any other age group.

Age of the Elderly

The age structure of the sample elderly is indicated in table 3.1. Out of 231 elderly, 53 (22.94 percent) are of the age group 70-75, 52 (22.51percent) are in the age group of 65-70, the same number of 43 (18.61 percent) elderly are in the age group of 60-65 and 80-85 years respectively. The other 27 (11.68 percent) are in 75-80 years age group and the rest 13 (5.62 percent) are 90 years and above. This goes to show that there is a decent proportion of the age to which the elderly belong.

Sex ratio of the Elderly

The male-female ratio taken in this study is presented in table 3.2. Out of the total 231 elderly, 115(49.78 percent) are males and 116 (50.21percent) are females.

Family Type of the Elderly

The type of a family - nuclear, joint and extended family - is an important aspect having a bearing on the well-being of the elderly. This factor often affects the nature and amount of support the elderly receive, status and prestige they enjoy and access to emergency help when required. In India, it is taken for granted that families are the most natural living habitat for people of all ages, including the old, frail and the disabled.

Out of the total of 231 elderly, a majority of them (as many as 187) is living in a nuclear type of family i.e.

living with their spouse and unmarried children. This is so because in Meghalaya, the nuclear type of family is generally practiced, unlike in other parts of the country. The other 40 elderly are living in a joint-family consisting of married daughter(s) and their families and another four elderly are living in an extended type of family, comprising of family members who stay unmarried.

Marital Status of the Elderly

Many of the elderly interviewed were unmarried. Out of the 231 elderly, 168 were married and living with their spouse. The widowed elderly constituted 55, five were unmarried, two were separated and one was a divorcee. It has been observed that the marital status of the elderly people greatly influences their life style, and losing the spouse in old age brings a very hard time in the passage of one's life. The living partner has to face all the problems of old age without anybody to share or understand.

Educational qualification of the Elderly

Out of the 231 elderly, a majority of them (197 elderly) was under-matriculate and 68 illiterate. Among the literates, 82 have passed or attended class I-V and 47 elderly have passed or attended class VI-IX. Among the other more qualified elderly, six had passed class XII, nine were graduates, one completed research work and another completed a professional course. The level of educational qualification was found to be very low and one of the main reasons, according to many of the elderly, was that *education in our time is not so much important as it is today. At our time, getting a job is no big deal. We can get a government job even when still in high school.* Others maintained that *because of poverty they could not afford to go to school or had to drop halfway.*

Occupation (last held) of the Elderly

An analysis based on the mode of occupation last held by the elderly was carried out in the study. A majority (74) of the elderly was cultivators/agricultural laborers. Many of them reared livestock. The males generally do heavier manual works in the field than the females. Besides, there were 50 elderly Government employees, 38 were running business, 25 were daily wage earner, 29 were house-wives, six elderly were carpenters, five were teachers, and among the four other elders were nurses, a church elder and a contractor.

Income of the Elderly

Out of the 231 elderly, about 82 received a monthly income of Rs1000-2500 each, 64 had an income of Rs2500-5000 each, 32 earned less than Rs1000 each, 12 had an income of Rs5000-10,000 each, and seven elderly secured a monthly income of between Rs10,000-15,000 each. Only one respondent received a total family income of Rs15,000-20,000 and above. A total of 32 elderly did not want to mention anything on this issue.

According to the study, it has been noted that generally the rural people, who are predominantly depend on agriculture, have much less opportunity of gaining access to secure regular income than those depend on other occupations. Hence, there is a vast difference between those working in the government sector and non-government sectors. A majority of the respondents, both the elderly male and female, raised income through agricultural labor on a daily wage basis during the agricultural seasons. Hence their income cannot be fixed and usually it varies from time to time.

Community of the Elderly

The elderly people in Meghalaya belong to different communities. Out of the total of 231 elderly, 94 were Garos, 91 were Khasis, 37(16.01 percent) are Jaintias, four were Bengalis, two were Nepalis, two Hajongs, and one Assamese. A majority of the elderly was drawn from the tribal population of the State comprising of the Khasis, Jaintias and the Garo communities.

Status of Old Age Financial Security

Important findings, including the status of old age financial security of the respondents have been listed below.

1. About 56 per cent of the respondents has reported that they are facing financial problem.
2. Elderly people face serious financial problem during the early years of their retirement from active life. It is perhaps because a time lag is needed to adjust their consumption and spending habits with their reduced financial status. Financial problem was found to be less pronounced among the people of very old age (above 75 years of old).
3. In Meghalaya, the elderly males face relatively more financial problem than their female counterparts. Matrilineal social formation may be the reason for this inter-sex disparity.

4. The problem of old age financial insecurity was found to be acute among the Garo respondents, moderate among the Khasis and less among the Jaintias.

5. It has been found that the problem of old age financial insecurity bears some inverse relationship with the educational qualifications of the respondents. The lesser the educational qualification, the higher is the magnitude of the problem of old age insecurity and vice versa. It is evident that education instills skills in individual. The higher the level of education, the better is the prospect of securing formal jobs and higher income. With formal sector jobs come old age security measures. Moreover, higher income enables individuals to save more for the old age and thereby reduces the financial dependency.

6. Occupations of the elderly in their active life largely determine their status of old age security. It may be noted that 84 percent of the elderly who was/is associated with cultivation faces financial problem. About 56 percent of the elderly who was/is associated with non-farming activities reported to have less financial problem. The female elderly, who were/are housewives, also face considerable amount of old age financial insecurity.

7. Education, occupation, income and old age financial security are all related. Better education enables an individual to set a better job and to earn higher income. The higher the

level of income, the better is the financial position of an individual at the old age. A few respondents having higher income reported to have financial problem.

8. It has been thus observed that the illiterates, self-employed, low-income groups are more vulnerable to old age financial insecurity than the literate and formal sector employees. Old age security measures need to focus this vulnerable section of the elderly.

Status of Health of the Elderly

Important findings related to the status of health of the elderly respondents have been listed below.

1. About 50 percent of the respondents reported to have health problems. It has been observed that with age, health problem increases. This is only natural as age reduces the vitality of human organism.
2. Contrary to the general believe that the elderly male suffer more from health problems than the female elderly maybe due to greater exposure of the former to the stress-related activities and unhealthy habits like drinking, smoking, etc., higher percentage of the elderly females in Meghalaya reported to have health problems than their male counterparts. This contradictory finding calls for a deeper investigation of the phenomenon.
3. Health condition of an individual has something

to do with his lifestyle. The life style of people is to some extent, influenced by the religious faith they follow. It has been observed that the followers of Catholic faith suffer less at old age than the followers of other faiths. While about 54 percent of the followers of indigenous faith reported to have health problems, this percentage among the followers of the Baptist, the Protestant and the Catholic faiths was 51, 48 and 25 respectively. However, practice of a particular faith may not explain the health problems of an individual fully. People's access to health care services, availability of quality health care providers, economic condition of the people – all these need to be taken into consideration.

4. Contrary to conventional wisdom, sample data exhibits a negative relationship between educational level and income on the one hand and health condition of the respondents on the other. It has been observed that higher the educational level and income, more the health problems. One probable explanation may be that higher level of education is associated with higher level of income and higher level of income is, in turn, associated with greater profligacy. Lavish spending leads to health hazards. However, this trend is not reflected while health problems are seen against occupation. For the trend to be consistent, we would expect that higher educational achievements would lead individuals to get formal sector jobs which bring them higher

income. And hence, more formal sector employees should also report health problems. But Sample data does not exhibit this pattern. In contrast, higher percentage of people engaged in farming reported to have health problems and less percentage of people engaged in formal sector (Government employees) reported to have health problems. A further study is needed to look into this apparent contradiction.

Psychological Status of the Elderly

Psychological status is defined in terms of subjective feelings like loneliness, feeling of neglect and unwanted, etc. If a person reveals that s/he has any or all of the above feelings, s/he is supposed to have psychological adjustment problem. Some important findings listed below:

1. It has been found that the elderly suffer from psychological adjustment problems particularly during the early years of their retirement from active life. This primarily happens due to the role erosion as described in chapter 1, as the elderly, immediately after their retirement, are stripped of various roles and duties, both at home and workplace. It is difficult for an individual to reconcile with this change in his/her roles. As time passes, s/he gradually adjusts himself/herself with the facts of life and hence experiences lesser psychological adjustment problems. These problems worsen with the elderly ageing further.

2. As the elderly are the store house of experience, society should device a mechanism in order to engage them in various community services and thereby providing them with alternative roles so that they can overcome the role erosion syndrome.

3. It has been observed that the elderly males more suffer from psychological adjustment problems than their female counterparts. Probably, for the women, role erosion is much less at old age.

4. Only 11 percent of the Garo elderly reported to have psychological adjustment problems. This percentage among the Jaintias and Khasis is 51 and 33 respectively. However, it is not clear whether better stress management environment built in the ethno-social systems of the respective ethnic groups or in systems of faiths is responsible for the variations in the pattern of psychological adjustment problems. For better understanding of this phenomenon, separate study on cultural anthropology needs to be undertaken.

5. As educated and well off people can better plan and manage their old age, they face lesser psychological adjustment problems. Percentage of people facing psychological adjustment problems decline with higher educational achievements. People with formal sector employment also exhibit lesser psychological adjustment problems at old age than people with informal occupations.

4

INFORMAL CARE GIVERS & FINANCIAL DEPENDENCY OF THE ELDERLY

4.1 Informal care givers and the welfare of the Elderly

Informal care givers are those who look after the elderly, take care of their health and provide them with shelter and emotional support when they retire from active life. Informal care givers constitute the family members- son, daughter, wife and relatives, near and distant. In every society, informal care givers are the prime source of support for the elderly. Individuals, in their productive phase of life, invest in the welfare of their family members and kith and kin, and, in turn, they expect that their sons, daughters, wives and other relatives will take care of them when age incapacitates them.

Some basic information on the informal care givers and the relationship the elderly maintain with them has been given below.

Whether the elderly have children-male/female

Majority of the elderly spoken to has children. Out of a total of 231 elderly interviewed, 226 have children and five elderly do not have any children. From the 208 elderly having male children, 54 have one male child each, 41 elderly have two male children each, 46 have three male children each, 34 elderly have four male children each, 10 elderly have five male children each, six elderly have seven male children each and one elderly has nine male children.

While questioning about the female children, out of a total of 215 elderly, 55 elderly have one female child each, 47 elderly have two female children each, 49 elderly have three female children each, 33 elderly have four female children each, while nine, four and two elderly have six, seven and eight female children each respectively.

Total number of children the elderly have

When asked about the total number of children the elderly have, it was found that out of 231 elderly majority of them, i.e. 47, have five children each , 31 have three children each, 26 have eight children each. The same numbers of 24 elderly each have six and eight children respectively, 20 elderly have seven children each, 19 elderly have two children each and 15 elderly have nine children each. The remaining 10 elderly have ten to twelve children each.

The family size is generally large. The present study has indicated that except for 13.71 per cent and 8.84 per cent of the elderly who have less than five children each, the rest i.e. 77.92 per cent of the 231 elderly has a total number of children ranging from 5-12 each.

Children Dependent

Many of the children are not dependent on the elderly and they constitute a total of 143 (63.27 per cent). However, 71 elderly have both dependent and non-dependent children. Another eight said that their children are still fully dependent on them and the rest four elderly said that their children have died. Though 63.27 per cent elderly has children who are not dependent on them, around 35 per cent elderly partially or totally has children who still depend on them for livelihood. This in itself is one psychological adjustment problem leading to stress, tension and other problems that the elderly face.

Number of dependent male/female child

There are 54 elderly who have male-children dependents on them. Out of them, 36 elderly have one male dependent each, 13 have two each, four have three each and one elderly has five male dependent. As far as the female-children dependents are concerned, there are 56 elderly who have female dependents, 30 have one female dependent each, 19 have two dependents each, five and two elderly have four and six female dependents each respectively.

Total number of dependent children

Therefore, as indicated earlier, in total there are 79

elderly whose children are dependent on them, 28 elderly have one dependent child each, 26 have two dependent children each, 14 have three each, seven have four each and two elderly have five and six children dependent each respectively. Whatever the numbers of dependents the elderly have, the fact is that they are still dependent on them.

Manner of dependency

The manner in which the children are dependent on the elderly has also been briefly described here. Of the 79 elderly whose children are dependent, 36 elderly have children who are still students, 31 have children who are unemployed, nine elderly whose children are both student as well as unemployed and the remaining three elderly have children who are handicapped. It has been found that the loss of income is sudden in the case of retired persons. They cannot but experience set back, particularly, if they have children and other dependents to support after their retirement.

Occupation of the children

The occupation of the children varies from teacher to government employees to those engaged in business, in agricultural activities and other off-farm activities (this does not include the children who are dependents). The occupation of the children involves a decent proportion. It has been observed that the majority of the children (i.e., 312 of them) is engaged in agriculture, 302 are working in various government departments and 261 are involved in business. The other 60 and 58 are housewives and teachers respectively, while the remaining children are involved in private, non-governmental, mission work etc.

Monthly income of working children in total

With the family size generally large, it is found out that the total income of the children in a family varies. Out of the 222 elderly family, 58 elderly have children whose total income range from 5000-10,000 each; 54 elderly have children who earn Rs 10,000- Rs 15,000 each; The income of children of 34 elderly is Rs 15,000-20,000 each; 29 elderly have children whose total income is Rs 20,000 and more each; 16 elderly have children with an income of Rs1000-Rs2500 each; The children of 15 earn Rs2500-Rs5000 each and the rest 14 elderly did not mention the total income of their children. The monthly income of the working children depends on the family size of the elderly. But it is found out in this study that the total income of the children of the elderly is quite low in comparison to the total number of working children in the family. For example, the 13.95 per cent of the elderly families has a total income of less than Rs 5000 a month, with a minimum of 5-6 members in each family.

Contacts with children living separately

The present study reveals that out of 214 elderly having children, a majority of the elderly (i.e. 199) is still in contact with their children living separately. Eight said that they had lost contact, while four said that they were still staying together with their children and the remaining three did not mention anything in this regard.

Reasons for leaving parents by children

There were various reasons cited for the children leaving their parents. In this study, out of 214 (100 percent) elderly, most of the (at least 61) elderly indicated that their children had had to leave them due to marriage, another 49 elderly said that it was both due to marriage and service, 37 said because of service, business as well as marriage, 30 elderly indicated that their children left them because of business and marriage. The rest have their own specific reasons like sickness, their children don't love them, and they want to stay separate and so on. However, it was evident that because of service or business, the elderly would be left alone in the village or towns to fend for themselves. This also applies to the parents whose children have migrated to other places.

Loneliness & Neglect

Out of the 231 elderly, 127 expressed their loneliness, sorrow or neglect, as they face various problems, while the remaining 104 elderly denied that they experience any such feelings.

Reasons for loneliness

While expressing the nature of their loneliness, they cited various reasons. One of the main reasons is the financial hardship faced by 38 elderly, followed by health problems cited by 13, and 12 struck by poverty. Ten elderly said they felt lonely for staying away from their children, nine said that it was because of family matters and six elderly said that they felt lonely because of the death of their spouse. The others indicated several problems, but mostly, it has been observed, the reasons for loneliness of the elderly were financial constraints, health problems and poverty. Some of the elderly stated that they felt lonely as they failed to receive proper attention and cooperation from their family members. They also complained of less attention and care from their family members than they used to get during their younger days. Some of them felt that they were a burden on their respective families.

Whether do any household works

With regards to household duties, 160 of the total elderly interviewed said they were involved in household activities, suggesting that they were still actively participating in the household works and 70 were reported as dependents. They need social assistance and support in their old age. The picture that emerges here is that most of the elderly keep themselves busy in household works. As many as 97 elderly still doing household works said that they received help from other members in the family. However, 35 elderly said that they were doing household works by themselves, many of whom include the elderly females.

Who take more care?

Out of 231 elderly, 89 elderly said that they received care from both their sons and daughters, 69 said that they received more care from their daughters, some said they received more care from their husband/wives, close relations, sons and so on. But it was found that in most cases it is the daughters who take more care of their elderly parents in Meghalaya.

If no child, whether staying together with relatives

Out of the total of 13 elderly who had no children either because they remained unmarried or their children were dead, nine elderly said that they are staying with their relatives like their niece/nephew and with their grand daughter.

The four elderly who are not staying with relatives have their own reasons and each have their own views like no more contacts, no relatives, don't want to put pressure on them and relatives don't accept them.

Attitude of family members/relatives towards the elderly

The attitude of the family members or relatives towards the elderly may be based on whether they see the elderly with sympathy, without sympathy or their attitude towards them is bad mannered. A total of 161 elderly said that they were treated with sympathy, 62 elderly said otherwise, i.e., not treated with sympathy; five others said that the attitude of their family members or relatives was bad mannered, while another few said they were treated sometimes with sympathy and sometimes without sympathy. Those elderly who expressed their dissatisfaction over the attitude and behaviour of the younger generation said that it was because of the influence of modern outlook and life styles among the young members of the community, even as the traditional norms and values were eroding fast. Interestingly, there was also deterioration in inter-personal relationship with their children, which was found to be severe in extremely old age. This might be due to greater dependence of the elderly on their children for meeting many kinds of needs. However, more than 60 per cent elderly opined that they have satisfactory relations with their family members.

With whom are they staying?

The living arrangement of the elderly is also an important factor in mitigating the problems of the elderly. This information would help in assessing the role played by the family. Living arrangements of the elderly has been categorized into living with wife/ husband, living with children, living with daughter/son, living with grand children, and living with close relation. In the study, it was found, most of the elderly constituting 107, was living with their daughters. This is may be because of the matrilineal tradition of the tribes in Meghalaya, where it is the duty and custom of the daughters to take care of their elderly parents. All together 28 elderly were found to be living with their spouses, 17 were living with wife and children, 14 with their children, 13 with their son and 13 others were living with both wife and daughter. There were also those who lived alone, or in an old age home or with grand children or with close relatives. In the past, older people were invariably staying with their close relatives, especially their children. But in the present day system, the character of family is fast changing. Such a change in family structure of younger family members seeking urban job opportunities are compelling an increasing proportion of older people to live by themselves or with spouse.

How are they treated?

All together 161 elderly indicated that they were

treated well whereas 66 said that they were ill-treated. Those who said that they were not happy with care and treatment offered their own views. Some said it was because of the inter-generational conflict, which, of course, is not a new phenomenon. There are countless issues that can transform into conflict. A simple issue may blow up into a major conflict when there will be no compromise between two members. Others said that it was due to the employment of the children that creates a lot of problems to the elderly. Because of work, the children move away to other places, leaving the old parents alone in their house as care taker of the property. In some cases, the old parents in the beginning received well-behaviour and treatment from all members of the family, but gradually they felt their presence was a burden on the family. All such problems are influencing the physical and mental health of the elderly to a great extent. They are not in a position to maintain their food, clothe, house and social amenities in good manner. Some of them are not in a position to say anything. Sometimes they are happy with the care given to them but in another time they complain of inadequate care from the family members. This frequent swing in behaviour among the elderly also affects the attitude of the family members towards the former. This may, in turn, upset the care givers when they begin to feel that their services are not appreciated by the elders.

Matrilineal tradition and customs ensure proper care and respect for the elderly. Agree/Disagree

Of the 231 elderly respondents, 142 agreed with the premise, 79 disagreed, 6 said that they have no idea, and the rest did not respond. It was found that many of the elderly agree with this view who believed that the elderly are still very much respected by their children or society, as they are regarded as advisors to the family in particular and society in general. Those who disagreed with the above statement said that nowadays the status accorded to the elderly is low, and some even said the present generation had no respect for the elderly persons. Some others asserted that there were changes in attitudes among the present generation of children, who appeared to be stubborn, less sensitive and at times rebellious, which shape their behaviour towards the elderly.

Neighbours aware of the elderly problems

A total number of 141 elderly felt that their neighbours were aware of the various problems they faced. The other 70 said that neighbours were unaware, 13 said that the question did not arise as they had no problems as such, while the remaining few did not respond to this issue. However, it was clear that in most cases, the neighbours were aware of the problems faced by the elderly.

Awareness about longevity

In a discussion about the awareness of longevity, 176 said that the elderly now live more than they did in the past, 27 said that they did not have any idea in this matter, 14 said that the life-span of the elderly in the past and present was more or less the same, while 13 elderly felt that the longevity of the elderly nowadays was less than the past. However, there was general unanimity among the elderly that the advancement of medical science and better health services and care facilities had certainly contributed to the longevity of people today.

Following are the findings that may be inferred from ground data

1. Informal care givers are the prime source of support for the elderly. Out of 231 respondents, nine have not mentioned as to with whom they are staying. As a result, our sample size in this case reduces to 222. About 97 percent of the elderly stay with their family members and relatives. Only two elderly said they stay alone. Out of 222, only four elderly were found staying at the Mercy Home, a care centre for the elderly. Thus, it can be said that generally the elderly in Meghalaya do not suffer much from familial and social isolation.

2. It has been noted that the average family size in Meghalaya is large. On an average, an elderly is having more than five children. We find hardly any relation between the informal care giving and the number of children a person is having. That is, having more children does not guarantee higher level of informal care. Moreover, we do not find any discrimination in informal care giving to the elderly across the sex of the children – male or female.

3. The matrilineal social system, which is prevalent among the Khasis, the Garos and the Jaintias,

vests the responsibility of care giving to the elderly upon the daughter in a family. Due to this, daughters play the crucial role in providing informal care to the elderly in Meghalaya.

4. It has been observed that rather than the number of children, the income level of children is positively correlated with the level of informal care giving to the elderly. The level of informal care giving is interpreted in terms of the attitude of the children towards the elderly. If the needs of the elderly are attended, it is interpreted as sympathetic attitude, if not, then, unsympathetic attitude. It has been observed that the higher the level of income of the children, more sympathetically the elderly is treated and the vice versa.
5. As the daughters generally bear the most of the responsibility of care giving to the family elderly and since the level of income of the children show positive correlation with the care giving, women's welfare should be focused adequately in the public policy. This will indirectly be beneficial for the welfare of the elderly in the long run.

4.2 Financial Dependency of the Elderly

There are broadly two categories of old people among the surveyed: (1) Those who have retired from active service and are in receipt of pensions and other benefits. They do not generally suffer from financial hardships. They are mainly in need of emotional and psychological support. (2) The other category of elderly comprising those who did not work for the government. They carved out a living just to keep their body and soul together. They continue to work as long as they are physically capable and retire when the advancing age has its full grip on them. They are often deprived of family support and left to themselves. Otherwise, their family is too poor to support them. A sense of insecurity and helplessness persists throughout the remaining days of their lives.

A brief analysis on the nature and extent of financial dependency of the elderly has been given below.

Financial dependence

The financial condition of the elderly at the last stage of their life is critical. Out of the total of 231 elderly, 120 were found to be financially dependent on their children, relatives or spouse. Most of them suffer from economic hardship. The other 111 were not dependent financially so much on their children and relatives.

If yes period of financial dependency

The period of financial dependency of the 120 elderly on their family, relatives or spouse, varies from person to person. Most of them, comprising of 54 were dependent for nine years or more, 19 each were dependent for three to five years and five to seven years respectively, 15 dependent for a period of one to three years, nine were dependent for seven to nine years and the remaining four were financially dependent on family, relatives or spouse for less than a year.

On whom financially dependent

As per the data, we find that most of the elderly

reported having means of subsistence from children with whom they are residing. The sample records that 67 of the 120 elderly are dependent on their daughter. This is more so because of the matrilineal type of system and custom in this society. Around 22 elderly are dependent both on their sons and daughters. Some said that they were dependent financially on their close relations and some said on their spouses work and savings. Thus older persons drawing their source of income from their children may create dissonant environment leading the younger generation to defy the older persons. Therefore, total or partial dependency may occasionally be subjected to inadequate facilities and abuse of the older persons.

On the other hand, the elderly who are expressing dissatisfaction with their lives are those who are financially dependent and generally they do not enjoy good health. A closer look indicates that they share strained relations with their family members as well. There are those who fail to receive adequate care and facilities from the family members. The people of this group are not economically productive because of their physical disabilities and some other reasons. The family considers them as a social burden and does not pay adequate attention to their needs. These elderly do not have much contact with friends and relatives and are often found in a miserable and neglected state. Amongst the poor, a greater degree of financial insecurity was noticed among the elderly. Weak financial position is one of the major problems of the Indian elderly. This makes their future insecure particularly in case of sickness or disability and financial worries have their bearing with social class.

Among the 111 elderly who are not dependent financially, most of them reported to have been receiving adequate protection from their family members. These elderly are economically productive by way of engaging themselves in one or the other domestic, business as well as agricultural activities of their respective families. They get proper attention, respect and protection from their family members. They are facing comparatively less difficulty. They enjoy their time and keep themselves engaged in several works.

Age of retirement from active life

Another significant aspect that emerged from the sample survey of the elderly was that at least 96 of them are still active in the sense that they are still earning their livelihood in one way or the other. They are engaged in business, agriculture and other works just to stay independent. This does not include the elderly who are in service. A total of 37 have retired from active work at the age of 70 years, 31 of them around 65 years, 18 around 75 years and 14 retired from active life at the age of around 80 years. They continue to work as long as they are physically capable of doing so. They are often deprived of family support and left to themselves. The other 21 elderly retired between 50 and 60 years. The rest 10 did not comment anything on this matter. It is interesting to note that, many are leading an active life and earning their own bread even after attaining the age of 60.

Reasons for retirement from active life

Majority of the elderly people suffer from economic hardships. Out of 135 elderly surveyed who no longer earn their living or who are no longer active, 67 elderly retired from active life due to old age. They said they wanted to work and not depend on anyone financially, but due to the old age, they had to quit. Another 12 elderly said they could not work anymore because of the sickness, while the other cited reasons of both old age and sickness. The remaining 15 did not respond. However, in most of the cases, old age and sickness are the main reasons for the elderly to retire from active life.

Age of retirement from service for working persons

On the question of retirement age from services for working persons, out of the total of 50 respondents, 27 elderly retired at the age of 58 years, 17 elderly retired after attaining the age of 60 years. This is so because the elderly did not give their actual age when they were recruited to the service. As a result, they are still in service even when reaching the retired age, but not officially. Six elderly retired before the retirement age due to problems such as sickness and accidents. It is important to note here that an abrupt fall in the income of the retiree is the most immediate and serious consequence of retirement from work. For the majority of the employees, obviously, the main source of regular income is their salary. As soon as an individual retires from his/her job, his/her income is reduced considerably. The retiree is then faced with the basic problem of meeting his/her daily needs and those of his/her dependents in the family. It was found that out of the

231 elderly only 50 were working in the government sector, while the rest 181 were engaged in agriculture, business, and other activities to earn their living.

Whether still active after 60 years of age

Data indicates that even after attaining the age of 60 years, at least 200 are still active and earning their living in whatever activities they were engaged with in order to support basically themselves or in some cases, their children who are still dependent on them. The other 31 elderly said that they were no longer active or earning after reaching 60 years. The elderly engaged in agricultural work, business and other works have no retirement age as such. This is the reason why they continue to be considered as economically active. In general, as old people move out of the labour force, either due to retirement or due to ill health and disability, their economic status suffers.

The elderly do contribute to the family either by helping in household chores or working for wages as domestic workers or as agricultural labourers or even dealing with business. The work output of the elderly against the expenditure incurred on their maintenance by the family members is a very sensitive issue, which, in a way, is a measure of respect that an elderly deserves. In our samples, not many people work in organized sector having well-laid out social welfare policies that keep them at a desirable socio-economic level throughout the rest of their life.

Whether received any pension or any other source of income

With regards to the question whether the elderly

receive any pension or any other source of income, 164 elderly responded positively indicating that they have access to money either from pension, savings of their own or from family members and close relations. There are also others owning a property and having financial investments which provide them security and a steady source of income. However, 66 elderly said that they have neither any pension benefit nor financial assistance from any other sources. Problems of the older persons who do not own productive assets have a somewhat varied dimension since old age brings dependency, absolute or relative and increases the burden on the family.

Those who depend on agriculture for their livelihood do not have worthwhile schemes for economic security during their old age. Of late, the old age pension has been introduced by the State Governments. But the quantum of such assistance is woefully meager.

Major findings

1. Majority of the elderly are financially dependent. This dependency increases with the advent of old age. With no stable inflow of income, they go on drawing whatever they could amass during their active working life.
2. Public intervention measures, hence, need to assign some age premium. The elderly who survive beyond the age of 80 are extremely vulnerable to old age insecurity. This age dimension needs to be factored into while deciding the amount of non-contributory social

welfare benefit that the government wants to provide to the senior citizens.

3. It has been observed that the elderly females are more dependent than their male counterparts. Out of 120 respondents who revealed that they are financially dependent, 62 percent of the female and 38 percent of the male elderly have reported financial dependency.

4. This variation across sex in terms of financial dependency also needs to be addressed. As the elderly females are more vulnerable to old age financial insecurity, gender premium should also need to be factored into while deciding the amount of social welfare benefits.

5. It has been observed that about 80 percent of the elderly associated with agricultural activities suffer from financial dependency. Only 39 percent of the elderly associated with non-agricultural activities has reported financial dependency.

6. This variation in financial dependency across occupational pattern also needs to be taken into consideration while framing welfare policy for the elderly.

7. Among the informal care givers, daughters play the most crucial role. In the matrilineal social system, the responsibility to take care of the elderly members vests on the daughter in a family. About 56 percent of the elderly in our sample fully depends on their daughters for financial and other support. Another 26 percent depends on their daughters partially.

8. As age progresses, more and more elderly retire from active life. This is obvious as ageing incapacitates them from doing physical work. Surprisingly, about 72 percent of elderly of the age group of 60-65 is still active. About 51 percent of the elderly of the age group of 65-70 also remains active.

9. It is, thus, obvious that the increase in longevity has made it possible for the elderly to continue to do work even till the mid 60s. This trend needs to be noted while formulating retirement policy. This indicates that there is a need for upward revision of the retirement age.

5

STATUS OF HEALTH OF THE ELDERLY : Health Problems and Health Care Services

The problems associated with old age and care of the elderly have not only socio-cultural and economic ramifications but also have bearings on the health and medical support systems. Ageing poses a major social challenge when vast resources are required to be directed towards the support, care and treatment of the old. With growing age, one starts to suffer from diseases and psychological problems. Older population is more vulnerable to morbidity and mortality. This chapter discusses the different health related problems of the elderly.

Facts relating to health problems of the elderly and their access to health care services have been analyzed and the findings listed below:

General Health Condition of the Elderly

Out of the 231 elderly people, 140 reported they were suffering from various kinds of diseases, whereas 49 elderly said they kept good health. Those who indicated that they enjoyed good health maintained that they did not have major sickness, but suffered from common cold, cough, fever and other minor sicknesses. However, 42 elderly said that their health status is neither good nor bad. Some of them said: *We sometimes enjoy good health but at times we suffer from various diseases. Therefore, we cannot say whether we are healthy or unhealthy.*

If bad, the kind of diseases suffered

At least 182 elderly said they suffer from various health-related diseases. As per data 37 suffer from high/low blood pressure, 31 from a combination of gastric, headache and symptoms of old age. The other 29 elderly suffer mainly from symptoms of old age like they cannot see, hear or walk properly. A total of 21 elderly have rheumatism, 12 have complained of heart disease and another 12 have diabetes along with blood pressure, 10 suffer from gastric problem and seven elderly suffer from asthma. At least 11 elderly suffer from tuberculosis, ulcer, typhoid, body pain and stomach problem. The remaining 12 elderly suffer from a combination of two or three diseases as mentioned above.

In the old age, it is noticed that rheumatism, heart problems, high/low blood pressure and diabetes, gastric was common among the people. During the old age, the immune system of the body weakens and it fails to fight diseases. They become ill due to the frequent attack of various diseases. One of the elderly said *even if I take medicines, they do not cure me completely. One day I may feel alright but the next day I feel sick again.* The old people tend to become home bound due to their dim eyesight, hearing deficiency and poor physique.

Type of treatment taken

The frequency of using health services is an indirect determinant of their state of health. An enquiry into the type of treatment taken in case of sickness reveals that out of the 182 elderly, 76 treat themselves at government hospitals or dispensaries and 45 take treatment from local medicine men. They follow the traditional treatment. Another 32 elderly said they generally consult private doctors, 10 treat themselves by allopathic medicines, seven take treatment from both private doctors as well as government hospital/ dispensary. It is also seen that many of the elderly have availed of the services of government hospitals and dispensaries for treatment of their ailments. The rest of the elderly rely on homeopathic or self-medication. But it is to be noted that though around 40-50 per cent avail of the government health care services, another half remains out of the government health services. The question arises what is the reason behind those not taking the government health services.

Reasons for not receiving treatment in the Government clinic

Out of the 182 elderly, 16 said that they avoided government hospitals/dispensaries because they had to wait a long time, 15 did not comment anything and 10 elderly said that the doctors did not attend them seriously. Another nine elderly said that they did not receive the proper medicines, eight said that they did not receive due attention, while four elderly said the hospital was far away. A number of 31 elderly emphasized a combination of these reasons-the doctors do not attend them seriously, do not supply the proper medicine and do not receive well attention. There are around 40 per cent who express dissatisfaction over the services offered by the government hospitals. However, another 87 elderly said they received treatment for their sickness or diseases from government hospitals/ dispensaries and they were satisfied with the kind of treatment given to them.

Whether required any personal assistance

Out of 231 elderly, a majority of 164 elderly said they required personal assistance in various basic necessities. The other 67 elderly said they did not need any assistance. Some of them informed that as long as they were fit, they would like to do things on their own and some informed that they were compelled to do on their own as there was no one to help. In this way, they expressed their own feelings and emotions.

If yes, type of assistance

The types of assistance include such services as looking after the physical needs of the old, helping to dress and bathe, nursing them when they are ill, household activities etc. Out of the 164 elderly who said they required personal assistance, 92 of them need assistance in household activities like cooking, marketing and doing odd jobs around the house, including household chores. A total of 27 elderly need company for walking, 21 require personal assistance for a combination of walking, bathing and household activities. The rest need assistance either for dressing, or bathing and hearing. Many elderly felt that it was the duty and responsibility of the younger members of the family to take care of them. The study found that the elderly suffer from one or more physical problems but majority of them are capable of taking care of certain tasks with the assistance of others.

If required, who gave assistance

Out of 164 elderly who required personal assistance, 74 elderly said were helped by daughters, 30 by both sons and daughters and 13 by maid servants. The other seven elderly were assisted by grandchildren, six of them by wife and five others were assisted by their respective husbands. The rest were helped either by niece, nephew or by two or more members in the family. The family members generally fulfill the needs of the elderly by giving assistance to them. The elderly get more help from the daughters and other female members being a matrilineal society. Where both the elderly married partners are alive, the spouse provides immediate care.

Period of physical/personal assistance

Out of the 164 elderly, 49 were physically dependent for one to three years, 46 were physically dependant or need assistance for three to five years. The number of those who required assistance for five to seven and nine years and above was 19 each. At least 14 elderly said they needed assistance for seven to nine years, while 17 others said they required assistance for less than a year. Therefore, there is no fixed period of physical or personal assistance, but it is observed from the study that majority of the elderly in this sample study requires personal assistance for basic needs of day to day life. This is provided by none other than their own family members.

Following are the major findings

1. Majority of the elderly suffer from health problems.
2. The health problems magnify with age. While 44 percent of the elderly of the age group of 60-65 has reported health problems, this percentage rises with the age and about 85 percent of the elderly of the age group of 80+ reported to have health problems. Thus, problem of health bears a positive relation with age. This is a general trend and Meghalaya sample shows no exception.
3. In contrast to general trend, the elderly females in Meghalaya face more health problems than their male counterparts. While 57 percent of the elderly males reported to have health problems, 65 percent of the female elderly reported the same.
4. Out of 181 elderly who specified the diseases from which they suffer it has been observed that about 91 per cent of them suffers from age-related diseases. Elderly associated with agricultural activities suffer less than those elderly associated with non-agricultural activities. Moreover, the

elderly females suffer less from age-related diseases than the male elderly.

5. Age related diseases like heart problems, blood pressure, blood sugar, asthma, rheumatism, etc., are most common among the elderly. Public health policy needs to be thoroughly informed of this trend so that public health care services can focus on the health problems of the elderly. Adequate infrastructure in terms of both men and materials need to be created in public health centers in order to cater to the needs of the elderly.
6. About 40 percent of the elderly who suffers from health problems have complaints about the quality of health care services provided by public health care providers. It appears that public health care providers need to be sensitized about the health care needs of the elderly. Public health policy needs to be informed of this ground realities.
7. It has been observed that the elderly of high income group prefer health care services from the private health care providers, whereas the elderly of low income group access services from the public health care providers. As majority of the elderly in our sample belongs to low income group, deterioration of public health care services directly impinge upon their welfare.
8. As with age, elderly become physically handicapped, it is difficult for them to access health care services available at far away places.

Public health policy should take this fact into consideration. Health care services need to be brought at the doorstep of such physically handicapped elderly. Introduction of mobile health care service and expansion of rural health care centers will go a long way in enhancing the welfare of the elderly.

6

SOCIAL CONCERNS FOR THE ELDERLY

This chapter deals with the social concerns for the elderly. It has already been noted that informal care givers are the prime source of support to the elderly in Meghalaya. Formal care giving through institutional support like old age home, non-governmental as well as community based organizations is still at its nascent stage. Nonetheless, it is important to know the perspectives of different organized sections of people as to how do they perceive the problems of ageing that the society is increasingly facing.

Here, we shall first look at the policies and programmes of the Government of Meghalaya towards the welfare of the elderly. Next, we shall report the views of the key informants that have been gathered in course of the field study.

The views, opinions, suggestions forwarded by the key informants are mainly based on subjective perceptions and not necessarily based on objective facts. Finally, we shall present the views of the elderly that reflect their expectations from the society.

6.1 Policies and programmes of the Government of Meghalaya towards the welfare of the elderly

Meghalaya, like other States in India, follows the National Policy on Older Persons framed by the Ministry of Social Justice and Empowerment (MSJM), Government of India (attached in annexure). Some aspects of this policy are mentioned below:

- The National Old Age Pension Scheme (NOAPS) was introduced on 15th August 1995 under the National Social Assistance Scheme. The State Government has implemented this scheme by paying Rs100 per month to the elderly. But the quantum of such assistance is woefully meager and payment is not regular. Sometimes payment is made only twice a year.
- Through the District Rural Development Agency (DRDA), the money under the NOAPS scheme is distributed to the blocks of respective villages but provided only to the BPL (Below Poverty Line) elderly.
- Most of the elderly do not collect the money because of the distant places they live in and they may end up paying more money on traveling to block offices than the amount they are entitled to receive as monthly old age pension.

- Free medical treatment of only Rs1200 in a lifetime is given to a selected few provided they give the utilization certificate. They must also need to obtain the age of 60 for women and 65 for men.
- The Arnapurna scheme is another benefit given to the elderly, i.e. the free distribution of rice from the Central Government through the supply section of the Deputy Commissioner Office. This scheme is functional for the elderly in Garo hills belonging to the BPL family. They are provided with 30kgs of rice, 200gms of oil, and 200 gms of dal. But this too is not regular, sometimes it is being provided once in three months.

6.2 Views, opinions and suggestions of the key informants on the problems and welfare of the elderly

Information based on discussions and in depth interviews gathered from numerous stakeholders, including the District Social Welfare (DSW), Deputy Commissioners' Office (DC), District Rural Development Agency (DRDA), Block Development Office (BDO), various charitable organizations, NGOs and prominent social workers, has been presented below.

District Social Welfare (DSW)

In **Shillong,** the capital of Meghalaya, the District Social Welfare officials spoke of the facilities of the Government concerning the elderly, which include medical treatment that is given only once in a life time to the BPL elderly. The second thing is the Old Age Pension scheme, which is made available to the people by the Block Development Office (BDO) in different blocks of the area of Meghalaya.

The DSW further informed that there was a decline in the status of the elderly in the family, and one of the reasons was the inter-generational conflict which seems to pose a threat to the respect and authority of the elderly.

In **Nongpoh**, the headquarters of the Ri-Bhoi district, the DSW informed that the elderly belonging to a BPL family was given a one time grant of Rs 1200 for medical treatment only once in a lifetime, provided the elderly produce the utilization certificate. It further indicated that there are grants and schemes for the elderly but no initiative has been taken to implement the schemes properly. In rural areas, there are many elderly who have none to care for them. As a result when sickness gets a hold on them, they die without anyone's concern. Therefore, it suggested that the government establish Old Age Home to take care of the neglected elderly persons.

In **Tura,** the headquarters of the West Garo Hills district, also the DSW emphasized the need for setting up Old Age Home for the elderly destitute. In **Baghmara**, the headquarters of the South Garo Hills district, the DSW informed that 10kgs of rice and 200gms of mustard oil were given to the elderly every month. The officials also informed that the one time grant of Rs 1200 for medical treatment was given only to the BPL families who are 80 years above. The DSW further said that in Baghmara there are elderly persons who live alone with no one to care for them especially during sickness.

The DSW in **Williamnagar,** the headquarters of the East Garo Hills district, said most of the people in the district were poor and they suffer frequently from various sicknesses which leave the elderly uncared. Hence, the government should provide Old Age Homes for such kind of people. It also implemented the one-time financial assistance scheme for medical treatment of the elderly belonging to BPL families.

Deputy Commissioner's Office (DC) - District Rural Development Agency (DRDA)

The DRDA in Nongpoh, Baghmara, Williamnagar, Jowai informed that Old Age Pension of Rs 100 per month was given to the elderly persons belonging to BPL families. However, they informed that this amount was not sufficient as most of the elderly who lived in far off places found it difficult to access the scheme as they had to bear the traveling cost which could not afford. That is why many elderly are not interested in receiving this pension. They suggested that the Government should increase the pension amount and implement housing facility for the elderly.

In Baghmara, the Annapurna Scheme by the Central Government for the free distribution of rice to the BPL families is also being implemented for the poor elderly persons. They receive 10kgs of rice monthly. But this distribution is not regular. It further informed that 25 to 50 per cent of the elderly in Baghmara is homeless, and therefore government must create housing facilities for them.

Block Municipal Board (BMB)

In Tura and Williamnagar, the BMB informed that

the Old Age Pension scheme is being provided to persons of 60 years and above but said that some do not avail of this because the amount is too small. Many of the elderly in these areas are generally poor, and even after attaining the age of 70-80 years, they need to work for sustenance. Therefore, the government should take some action to see that this section of the population is taken care of.

Block Development Office (BDO)

In Nongstoin, the headquarters of the West Khasi Hillsdistrict, the literacy rate among the elderly persons is very low. Many of them are daily wage earners and even after attaining the age of 60 years also, they continue to work as long as their body permits them. Though, they are aware of the Old Age Pension, they are not satisfied with the amount as it does not meet their basic needs. The BDO informed that many elderly suffer from various diseases as they do not take proper care of themselves. Thus it was felt that besides an Old Age Home, awareness of health education is also very much needed.

Education Department (Additional Secretariat) - Shillong

The department has plans to introduce in the curriculum aimed at creating awareness among the students about the importance of the elderly and respect that they deserve in the society. It further felt that continuing education should be encouraged for the elderly, in the form of creative art and culture, writing books or magazines. The elderly could then utilize their knowledge, experience and talent for the benefit of the society as a whole. Seminars and conferences regarding issues related with the elderly should be held with the participation of the elderly. With regards to the Old Age pension, it informs that such an amount is too less given the high cost of living nowadays.

Charitable Organisations

Mercy Home-Shillong

This is the only Old Age Home in Meghalaya which caters exclusively to the needs of the elderly persons. Since its inception in 1973, the Home has been taking care of the elderly who are destitute, sick, poor, widowed and the ones deprived of the basic necessities of life and human dignity. Elderly persons from different parts of the State seek accommodation here. It started off with a few elderly but now it has reached its maximum capacity and cannot accommodate anymore. What is now a matter of grave concern is the fact that the number of such helpless elderly is on the rise, and they need shelter and care. The Home authority felt that unless the Government stepped in and created support system for the poor and destitute elderly, Mercy Home alone would not be able to deal with the situation.

Missionaries of Charity-Shillong

This organization takes care of the young and old alike. Elderly persons who are destitute, poor and sick are taken care of and provided with free medical treatment, food, clothing and shelter. According to this organization, though the elderly are taken care of properly, most of them suffer from socio-psychological problems. They require love, respect and appreciation from their family members. It further informs that there are elderly persons being brought here by their own family members either because of poverty or sickness or because of both poverty and sickness.

Therefore, it suggested that the government should have mobile clinics to take care of sick elderly people; it should have various programmes to encourage relatives and children to take care of their parents and in return the parents take care of their children.

St Saviour Society of Jesus Christ- Tura

This organization informs that it takes care of the elderly who are genuinely sick and poor. In doing so it provides them with mid-day meal and involves them in repairing or other activities such as making mats, brooms, canes and others. These are then sold in the market and the money received goes directly to the fund for the elderly. The elderly come from their own respective homes and spend their day with this organization. It further informs that the purpose of this organization is to prevent the old persons from begging and take to the streets. There are many elderly persons who have been ignored and left by their families. Hence it suggested that there should be hospitals like nursing homes which take exclusive care of the elderly during their sickness. It also suggested that younger generation should be taught to respect their parents especially in old age, Old Age Pension is too less an amount and concessions should be given to the elderly by producing identity cards whether in traveling, medical treatment, essential items and so on.

Meghalaya Parents Association for Disabled (MPAD) - Shillong

The young and old alike are provided with some facilities by this organization. For the elderly, crutches, hearing aid and free medical treatment are provided, but only to a few. This is because the State Government has not taken seriously the schemes like Persons with Disability (PWD) implemented by the Government of India. The MPAD expresses that till date, the Government could not provide such facilities to the elderly. And if medical facilities could have been provided, the life-span of the old people would have improved much. Therefore, the Government should take a serious note of this issue.

Non-Governmental Organisations (NGOs)

Impulse Network-Shillong

According to the president of this organization, there is a growing need in Meghalaya to take care of the elderly persons. This is in view of the fact that there are many elderly who come and ask for jobs at this centre. She felt that the problems that the elderly face were mainly due to change in family structure; nowadays the number of nuclear families is increasing, as the younger generation is moving out of their homes in search of employment and better opportunities.

She suggested that facilities like the Old Age or Nursing Homes, Recreational Centre for the elderly should be created, and the BPL elderly should have special concessions such as increase in amount of old age pension.

Kripa Foundation- Shillong

This organization stresses on the importance of the family to play a key role in avoiding various problems of the elderly. It is the role and responsibility of the children to take care of the elderly when the parents had already taken care of them earlier. The elderly need human affection more than anything else.

Drop-In Centre- Jowai

Expressing the need of an Old Age Home or a Nursing Home, this Centre informs that because of poverty the families of the elderly are unable to take care of them. Therefore better provisions like free medical treatment, support for meeting basic requirements and a separate queue for the elderly in banks, offices and other public services should be thought of.

Mothers' Union-Baghmara

The Old Age Pension scheme provided by the Government is not sufficient. It further stressed the need for old age Homes for those elderly who have none to care for them.

Social Worker- Shillong

The emerging nuclear families and the compulsion of the children to go out to other places in search of jobs and businesses, are adversely affecting the elderly and their care support system within the family. A social worker during a conversation with the field research team observed that the elderly should be provided with both financial and psychological support. Old age homes or Nursing homes with counselors should be provided and the Old Age Pension scheme should be revised as the amount received by the elderly is too less.

Community Worker-Shillong

A retired nurse who is actively involved in helping the poor and needy through her church made the following observation: In the matrilineal society, the role of a father is less important than the uncle. The authority of a father is limited within his own family and this slowly and gradually alienates him as he grows old. She suggested that there should be programmes, workshops or seminars regularly for the elderly so that they can participate and voice their grievances. The Old Age Pension scheme also should be regularly distributed.

Conclusions

To sum up, following are the views and opinions of the key informants on the problems of the elderly and suggestions how to address them:

Problems

- Old age pension and medical treatment are too meager an amount. The schemes have not covered all of the needy elderly especially those belong to the BPL families.
- It has been learnt that only few elderly have availed of these services, and one of the reasons being that these are utterly inadequate.
- Even after attaining the age of 60 years, many poor elderly are compelled to keep on working as long as they can.

- There are many elderly persons who have none to care for them and so many of them seek accommodation in charitable organizations like Mercy Home in Shillong.
- The Government has not been able to provide the elderly with adequate health care services. If medical facilities were made available to the elderly on time the life-span of the old people would have improved.

Suggestions

- There should be proper implementation of schemes and policies from the State Government on the elderly.
- Amount of pension and medical treatment should be increased.
- There should be a uniform social security system for the elderly and the procedure in receiving it should be made simple.
- More Old Age Home or a Nursing Home to take care of the elderly persons should be set up in each district in Meghalaya. The State Government should encourage NGOs or CBOs with financial assistance to run Homes or centers for the elderly not only for old-age care but also for their recreations.
- The elderly should be able to access the concessions easily and comfortably offered to them for various purposes such as traveling, medical treatment and essential items especially for the

BPL elderly. For that purposes, the elderly could be given identity cards that includes proof of age.

- A separate queue for the elderly in banks, offices and other public services should be provided.
- There should be programmes, workshops or seminars regularly for the elderly so that they can participate and voice their grievances.
- The Government should take immediate steps to take care of the elderly before the situation is blown out of proportion.

6.3 Views, opinions and suggestions of the Headmen, Social workers (SW), Non-Governmental organisations (NGOs) and community workers (CW) on the problems and welfare of the elderly

A total of 82 important individuals/ resource persons involving headmen, NGOs, community and social workers, were contacted who had given their views, opinions and suggestions on the problems of elderly population. Among them 20 were headmen, 25 social workers, 22 community workers and 15 NGO functionaries. The research investigators while doing the field study consulted with them. This consultation is purposely made in order to understand their level of awareness, attitudes and behaviour towards the elderly. It may be noted that though the Headmen, SW/CW or NGOs have expressed their views, opinions and suggestions for the various schemes and policies to be implemented for the elderly, we have presented only those preferred by the majority.

Type of Facilities

Out of the 22 CW and 20 Headmen, 15 and 11 respectively, were of the view that there should be a combination of Old age allowance, Government housing facility in the form of an old age home or nursing home, recreation facilities, health services & free traveling fare from the Government. Out of the 15 NGOs, seven spoke of old age allowance and health services. The SW consisting of 10 out of 25 individuals recommended Old age allowance only.

Types of programs to be adopted for elderly

Many of the CW, headmen, NGO and CW agree on the other aspects, like community's help, awareness of health education in the area or locality, health facilities and educating the younger generation in taking care of the elderly. Few agreed on recreational facilities.

Type of facilities to be adopted for those who have none to look after them

For those elderly persons who have none to take care of them, the recommendations include government housing, financial benefits, social help, regular monthly ration and free medical treatment. From these facilities, the government housing in the form of an old age home or nursing home was recommended by seven CWs, seven headmen, five NGOs and eight SWs. This is because the elderly will be well looked after in all aspects right from their basic needs if they are kept in this kind of accommodation provided by the Government.

What should be done for ailing elderly

On the issue of "what should be done for sick elderly

people", many are of the view that a nursing home is the need of the hour in which sick elderly people can stay for a considerable period of time until they are cured. This is required because, according to them, when a person becomes old and sick, his recovery is slow. The hospital cannot keep such people for a long time. They have to discharge the elderly even when they are not in a position to walk. Hence, the government should provide for nursing homes or even nursing facilities at home. Hence, seven CW, six Headmen, five NGOs and five SWs felt the need for a nursing home.

The facilities like arrangement to take them to the hospital, mobile care services at home and free health services are also considered as vital in taking care of the elderly. These will make the burden a lot lighter for the relatives or family members who take care of the elderly, in case anything bad happens to the elderly.

To sum up, it has been observed that besides the old age allowance, recreation facilities, health services & free traveling fare from the government, majority of them highly recommended establishment of nursing homes and an old age homes. Keeping in mind the difficulty of the family members especially the poor in taking care of the sick elderly and also the increasing number of the destitute elderly, such homes provided by the government will be ideal. By doing so, it will very much lighten the burden of the family members, especially those belonging to the BPL families, to a large extent.

6.4 Opinions and suggestions of the elderly on care and support system

Opinions and suggestions of the elderly were also

taken to understand their perception on the advantages and disadvantages of being old, preferred living arrangements, community involvement and their specific needs. Here however, we shall focus on those aspects which are felt by the majority.

Out of the 231 elderly surveyed, 70 felt that the government should provide them with housing facilities, old age pension and free medical treatment. This in itself shows that they are not aware of the old age pension scheme. All together 46 said that the government should set up old age home for those who have none to look after and provide for free medical facilities. They further stated that the old age pension should be increased so that they can at least support themselves.

Another 26 elderly said that they could not specify anything in particular but informed that the government should recognize the various problems faced by the elderly and therefore should extend help and support to them in any way possible, while 16 elderly stressed the need for financial assistance so that they could meet some of their basic requirements.

At least 10 elderly said that there should be free medical treatment for the elderly and other health facilities and 10 others who are disease-ridden and unable to move, wished the government provided facilities for health care services in their own respective homes. The need for nursing home or old age home especially for those who have none to care for them was also reiterated by another 10 elderly.

The other eight felt that free medical treatment should be given to the old persons, seven wanted certain special consideration for those who are above 60 years that they do not have to stand long in a queue while availing of the public utilities. At least four elderly said that the government should give free medical treatment and free traveling fare for the elderly above the age of 75 years, while four talked about regular monthly ration and another four wished that the elderly enjoyed better status, respect and authority in the family as well as in the society.

Some were of the opinion that the government should provide assistance to every elderly and not only to the Below Poverty Line (BPL) families, others maintained that the government should promote awareness of health education in the area and also recreation facilities and so on. In addition, two elderly said, *the State Government should sincerely implement all facilities already provided by the Central Government and the state government should conceive its own policy for providing other facilities.* Another elderly said *75 per cent of state schemes for the elderly such as, the old age pension and 25 per cent of the Central scheme remained non-operational in the State.*

In short, majority of the elderly felt that the government should provide housing facilities like old age homes, old age pension and free medical treatment. This shows that they are not aware of the old age pension scheme and even if they were, they felt the scheme was not useful at all as the amount was very small. The other suggestions were financial assistance, health care services in their own respective homes, free traveling fare, regular monthly ration, awareness of health education in the area and so on.

Conclusion

The present study shows that many of the elderly are unaware of their rights as senior citizens as well as the government policies and services available for them. Lack of awareness, low literacy level, absence of proper guidance from the government officials, lengthy procedures involved in accessing the benefits and irregular pension services are major reasons cited by the elderly for not availing of the benefits. Even those who are aware of such programmes are not able to avail of the benefits due to difficult procedures. Many of them opined that government programmes, because of lack of transparency and lengthy procedures, failed to fulfill the needs of the older people. The state government and the department concerned need to address all these issues, review implementation procedures and take appropriate measures to improve health and support care systems for the elderly in Meghalaya.

7

CONCLUSION : Recommendations and Suggestions

Advances in medical sciences have contributed to healthier and longer life, even as giving rise to an increasing ageing population. Ageing has different implications for different groups of people in different countries. It means more wealth and enhancement of power for some and forced retirement and dependence on provident fund or pension for the other. For many others, ageing means a state of total dependence and living in abject poverty. The present study has shown that the number of elderly is increasing rapidly. The population of 60+ is assuming an enormous size. The rise in population of the elderly and its growing proportion in the total population is creating new problems for the society and for themselves. The resulting problems posed by the increasing number of elderly persons in the population will increase substantially in future, which deserve immediate attention.

The Constitution of India in its Directive Principles has accorded special importance to the well being and care of the elderly. Since the Eight Five Year Plan, the Government of India has initiated a number of welfare schemes for the elderly. The willing voluntary and non-governmental organizations have been given financial assistance to set up old age homes, day-care centers and implement various programmes for the elderly. The Ministry of Social Justice and Empowerment (MSJE), has also been implementing a number of schemes for the aged/elderly since 1992 as per the *National Policy on Older Persons*, MSJE, Government of India (attached in the annexure).

The concept of old age is not same throughout the world. Likewise, in Meghalaya too, there is no clear cut definition of the elderly. Different scholars have different views and opinions on the elderly but from various definitions of old age, they all seem to agree that becoming old is associated with the later part of life of an individual in which symptoms of physical deterioration begin to appear. In this study, persons aged 60 years and above have been defined as the elderly.

In the matrilineal tradition of Meghalaya, where the family and kinship ties are said to be still strong, it is generally believed that the elderly face much less problems than their peers do in other communities. The responsibility of looking after the old family members is taken for granted. They spend their last days with their family and kin groups who often need their advice and guidance. They are treated with honour and respect, and thus well integrated in the society.

However, this trend is gradually changing with the deepening of forces of modernization. Traditional values are giving way to the predicaments of modern living, life style and material persuasion. Therefore, the informal care taking system built-in traditional social and family structures is gradually fading away.

The emerging stresses and strains arising out of emerging urban culture and pursuit of modern lifestyle are also affecting the social and family structures, resulting in the gradual decline of role and status of the elderly in the society. With gradual increase of the elderly population and with more and more children unable to take care of their parents due to various reasons such as poverty, sickness and job opportunities, there is a growing population of destitute elderly in the age group of 60 and above. The situation is most likely to deteriorate in the years to come.

The respect for the elderly is slowly eroding even in the rural areas. Inadequate financial resources, poverty and sickness continue to be the major problems of many of the elderly, which need to be addressed. Old age is generally accompanied by a number of problems that the elderly have to endure. Loss of economic independence and physical vigour and the emergence of various types of degenerative diseases change an elderly from an independent, self-supporting individual to one who needs help from his children, members of the family and the society in general. After an active and productive phase of their lives, they suddenly find themselves socially marginalized. The society is undergoing a phase of social transition, and the traditional caring and according status to the elderly is vanishing slowly. No wonder, they find themselves neglected, helpless and rendered useless.

General Trend of the Elderly Population in Meghalaya

- Elderly population in Meghalaya is growing at a faster rate than the overall growth of population.
- While the decadal growth rate of population has been 30.65 percent during 1991-2001, the same for the elderly population stands at 34.27 percent.
- Growth of the elderly population is not evenly distributed across the State.
- Growth of the elderly population is concentrated in three districts, viz., Jaintia Hills, West Khasi Hills and East Garo Hills.
- Rural Meghalaya bears much of the burden of the elderly population than its urban counterparts.
- While in 1991, longevity at age 60 for female was higher than the males, this gap has been reduced in 2001.

Socio-Economic Status of the Elderly

Meghalaya has a large section of poor elderly population and they live in miserable conditions. Those who retired from the government services may be a little better off than the general elderly population, which does not have regular sources of income, including pension benefit. Many of such elderly try their best to keep themselves economically productive as long as possible in order to lead a dignified life within the family and society. The economic condition of the elderly in a society often determines the nature of the treatment they deserve to receive. Therefore, the elderly, especially those who have become inactive and financially dependent, are perceived as a burden on the family and the society in general, as the economic status has a bearing on the social status of the older persons.

Trends in Socio-Economic Status of the Elderly in Meghalaya

- About 56 per cent of the respondents has reported to have financial problems.
- Elderly people face more financial problem during the early years of their retirement from the active life. It is perhaps because a time lag is needed to adjust their consumption and spending habits with their reduced financial status.
- The elderly males face relatively more financial problem than the elderly females, perhaps, due to the prevalence of the matrilineal social system among the tribal communities.
- The problem of financial security among the elderly is acute among the Garos, moderate among the Khasis and the least among the Jaintias.
- The problem of financial security bears some inverse relationship with the educational levels

of the respondents. The lesser the educational levels, the higher is the magnitude of the problem of old age security and the vice versa.

- Illiterates, self-employed, low-income groups are more vulnerable to old age financial insecurity than those who are literate, formal sector employees and high income group people.
- Majority of the elderly is financially dependent. This dependency rises through ages of the elderly.
- Self-employed elderly particularly associated with agricultural activities are found to suffer from financial dependency more than their counterparts associated with non-agricultural activities.
- Majority of the elderly depend on their daughters for financial support.
- The increase in longevity has made it possible for the elderly to continue to do work even till the mid-Sixties.
- A large number of the elderly suffers from psychological problems particularly during the early years of their retirement from active life. This primarily happens due to the role erosion, as the elderly immediately after their retirement are stripped of the various roles and duties, both at home and workplace.
- The elderly males suffer more from psychological problems than their female counterparts. It is probably because, for the women role erosion is much less at old age than the males.

- The elderly among the Garos suffer the least from psychological problems. The Khasi elderly suffer moderately, while the Jaintia elderly suffer the most.
- Educated elderly suffer less from psychological problems than the uneducated ones do.
- Informal care givers (family members and relatives) are the prime source of support for the elderly.
- No trend is found between the number of children and the level of informal care giving.
- Daughters particularly the youngest ones play the crucial role in providing informal care to the elderly in Meghalaya. It is mainly because the matrilineal social system, which is prevalent among the Khasis, Garos and Jaintias, vests the responsibility of care giving to elderly with the daughter in a family.
- The income level of the children, instead of their number, is found to be positively correlated with the level of informal care giving to the elderly.

Status of Health of the elderly and their Access to Health Care Services

Becoming old is a process which gradually damages the organism and reduces its vitality. There is a close connection between ageing and morbidity. The study shows a significant association of age with respiratory problems and other common diseases specific to the ageing process, i.e., rheumatism, diabetes, high/low blood pressure etc.

Health is one of the major problems faced by the elderly. As many as 50 per cent of the respondents suffers from various health related issues like high/low blood pressure, rheumatism, diabetes, gastric, old age symptoms and so on. Even when one is not suffering from any diseases, s/he experiences gradual decline in physical strength with the growing age. It is observed that they do not take much care of their health. Health practices are not well developed and around 70 per cent of the elderly in this sample requires personal assistance for various basic needs either physically or in household activities. The family members and especially the daughters, generally fulfill the needs of the elderly by giving assistance to them.

Trends

- Majority of the elderly reported to have health problems.
- A higher percentage of the elderly females in our sample has been found with various health problems than their male counterparts.
- In the Jaintia hills, the elderly have been found to be suffering the most from health problems, followed by the Garos in the Garo hills and the Khasis in the Khasi hills.
- Contrary to conventional wisdom, sample data exhibits a negative correspondence between the educational level and the income on the one hand and the health condition of the respondents on the other.

- Health problems magnify with age.
- Age-related diseases like heart problems, blood pressure, blood sugar, asthma, rheumatism, etc., are most common among the elderly.
- Elderly associated with agricultural activities suffer relatively less than their counterparts associated with non-agricultural activities.
- A large section of the respondents (40 per cent) who suffers from health problems has complained of non-availability of quality public care services.
- The elderly with high income prefer health care services from the private health care providers whereas those with low income access the same from the public health care providers.

Social security measures available to the elderly of Meghalaya

The elderly face four major problems. First is the problem of financial security; Second, the health problems; Third, the psychological problems, and finally, the problems arising out of physical inability. They need support to cope up with all these problems. With increasing inability of the informal care givers to look after the interest of the elderly and with rising share of elderly to total population, the quality of life of the elderly is showing gradual erosion. In fact, they are the most vulnerable among the destitute. There is, thus, an urgent need for strengthening formal care-giving facilities for the elderly. The State has to step in to create adequate infrastructure to deal with the problems that the elderly are facing. State intervention can radically improve the quality of life of the elderly.

Status of the Social Security measures available for the elderly in Meghalaya is presented below.

- The Government of Meghalaya does not have yet a separate policy for the elderly and their social security. Of course, it recognizes the need for a policy on the elderly.
- Currently, the State government through its department of social welfare is only implementing the National Policy on Older Persons framed by the Ministry of Social Justice and Empowerment, Government of India.
- However, the State is partially implementing the National Old Age Pension Scheme. Under the NOAP Scheme, all the elderly belonging to the BPL families are entitled to receive an amount of Rs100 per month as old age pension.
- There is also a provision for a one-time financial assistance of Rs 1200 given to the BPL elderly for medical treatment. Both the schemes, that is, the NAOP and the medical grant, are being implemented by the Department of Community and Rural Development, Government of Meghalaya.
- Besides, a provision is there under the Arnapurna Scheme for free distribution of specified amount of daily necessities like rice, edible oil, dal etc. to the BPL elderly.

Recommendations and Suggestions

Based on the findings described through the Chapters1-6, following recommendations and suggestions may be forwarded for the considerations of the society at large and the Government of Meghalaya in particular.

Old Age Security

1. It is impossible for any government to provide for adequate and full-proof old-age security in view of the enormous cost involved in supporting a growing population of the elderly. However, the Government can provide a bare minimum financial support. It can create market and non-market instruments and encourage people to plan and save more for the old age. It can also undertake a separate study in order to find ways and options, which could encourage people to save more during their active life.
2. Eligibility conditions for the old age pension need revision. Amount of pension should be inflation-adjusted. The base amount needs upward revision.
3. The transaction cost of pension needs to be reduced.
4. The delivery mechanism needs to be simplified and accessibility of the elderly needs to be improved.
5. Awareness campaign needs to be strengthened so that elderly in remote areas can avail of the existing schemes.

6. Whatever limited old age assistance programmes are available, their distribution should focus on the self-employed, illiterate and rural elderly who are most vulnerable to old age insecurity.

Health Care Services

7. Health care services offered by both the public and private health care providers need to be improved. Not that all the elderly depend on the public health facilities. For example, as per the information provided by the respondents, the elderly in the Jaintia Hills face less financial problem and they have the option of accessing both the public and the private health care services.
8. Public health care providers need to be sensitized and made more accountable to the needs of the elderly.
9. Public health care services need to be strengthened for the elderly with special units in hospitals and assured supply of medicine. It is also important to examine various models of health care so that the system can be improved.
10. Health centers exclusively for the elderly can also be considered. Health check ups and other related services need to be provided at the doorsteps to those who are immobile. Mobile medical services can go a long way in this regard.
11. Primary health centers need to be revitalized.
12. Health awareness programmes have to be

intensified, and in these efforts, the NGOs and the community-based organizations/clubs could be vigorously involved.

13. Public health care institutions need to be provided with adequate infrastructure – in terms of expert professionals, equipments and medicines – in order to deal with age-related diseases from which the elderly suffer.

Psychological Support

14. Informal care givers provide the psychological support to the elderly. Society needs to be sensitized about the problems of the elderly. This may be done through both formal system of education and informal socialization process. The State Government may carry out various public awareness campaigns about the problems and needs of the elderly by involving schools, the community-based organizations, traditional institutions and NGOs to disseminate the same.

15. It may also take initiative to introduce Social Service as part of the school curriculum and encourage the younger generation to help and serve the elderly in the surrounding areas.

16. Government may declare a day for the elderly population and encourage various social institutions and Civil Society organizations to observe the same. Artists, musicians, intellectuals, local celebrities and community leaders may be invited to join such programmes

to sensitize people on that day about the need for care of the elderly.

17. The elderly also should be encouraged to participate in various Social and Community works as they are the store house of experience and knowledge. This will make them feel happy, wanted and useful to the community life.

18. Even though the educated elderly are expected to cope with the retired life and the associated psychological stress better, government should focus on campaigns to expand adult literacy in the rural areas, where the majority of the elderly population lives.

Institutional and Policy Support

19. One of the key findings in the study was that many elderly respondents said they did not know of any scheme, such as, old-age pension or one-time medical assistance for those belonging to the BPL. And many of those who said they knew about the schemes were not availing themselves of the schemes either because the procedure was difficult and time-taking or the amount was too small. In order to address these problems, the government may consider the following: a) create a data base of the elderly population (village wise), identify the BPL families and enlist those elderly who are entitled to the existing two schemes, old-age pension and one-time medical grant. A village-wise household list has already been computerized by the C&RD, which is

available online; b) the identified BPL elderly in each village may form an SHGs, which will ensure that the money reaches the identified beneficiaries and records/books are maintained properly; c) Another option may be the use of tiny cards, a no-frill account scheme aimed at facilitating micro-credit to poor farmers, which is being promoted by the SBI to fulfill its mandate of financial inclusion. The tiny card, just like the ATM/debit card, contains the biometric information, a digital picture of the account holder and his/her thumb impression, which authenticates the identity of the individual account holder. The same kind of no-frill accounts can be made available to the identified elderly. The government may just transfer the old-pension amount to their account, which the elderly can access through the tiny cards at their convenience. A method may be worked out to update the list of surviving elderly NOAP beneficiaries once in a year or half-yearly basis. This will ensure transparency and full implementation of the schemes.

20. Besides, a reliable database on the health status, mortality and disability in terms of sex, locality and socio-economic status needs to be developed.

21. A review of the existing old-age support and care systems in the State, Community and family levels has to be carried out so that the gaps could be addressed and schemes improved.

22. Institutional care like Old Age Homes and

Nursing Homes for the elderly needs to be promoted and improved.

23. As the level of family income and not their number is positively correlated with the status of elderly care, society needs to be sensitized to restrict the family size so that parents can invest more in less number of children. More investment in children will make them better educated, which will enable them to get better jobs and secure higher income. This will then help the family take better care of the elderly.

24. Finally, the government may consider upward revision of the retirement age of the employees, as the elderly nowadays remain active till mid-Sixties because of better health care and advancement of medical sciences and technology.

25. Media can play a very important role in sensitizing the society about the problems of elderly and their needs.

BIBLIOGRAPHY

Akundy, Anand.2004. *Anthropology of Aging: contexts, culture and implications*. Serial Publications: New Delhi.

Atal, Yogesh. 2001. 'The United Nations and Ageing' in: Sharma, K L. *Indian Journal of Gerontology*, Quarterly Journal devoted to research on Ageing, 15(1-2). Rawat Publications: New Delhi.

Bali, Arun. 2000. *Bio-social Dimensions of Aging*. Indian Institute of Advanced Study Rashtrapati Nivas: Shimla.

Batra, Sharma. 2004. 'Health Problems of the Elderly- An Intervention Strategy' in: Sharma, K L. *Indian Journal of Gerontology*, Quarterly Journal devoted to research on Aging, 18(2). Bhalotia Publications: Jaipur.

Bazo, Maria-Teresa.2001. 'Family and Community Care for Elderly People in Spain'. in: Sharma, K L. *Indian Journal of Gerontology*, Quarterly Journal devoted to research on Ageing, 15(1-2). Rawat Publications: New Delhi.

Bhawsar, R D. 2001. 'Population Ageing in India: Demographic and Health Dimensions'. *Indian Journal of Gerontology*, 15(3-4).

Census of India. 2001. *Primary Census Abstract* -Tripura, Meghalaya, Assam & Sikkim.

Curran, Daniel J. and Claire M. Renzetti. 1993. *Social Problems*. Allyn and Bacon: Boston.

Dandekar, Kumudini. 1996. *The Elderly in India*. Sage Publications: New Delhi.

Dave Parul and John Ginu. 2003. 'A Look into the Lives of Older Persons' in: Sharma, K L. *Indian Journal of Gerontology*, Quarterly Journal devoted to research on Ageing, 17 (1-2). Kamal Publications: Jaipur.

Desjarlais Robert, Leon, Byron and Arthur Kleinman. 1995. *World Mental Health: Problems and Priorities in Low, Income Countries*. Oxford University Press, New York. 1995.

Donahue, Wilma. 1960. 'Housing and Community Services', in: Ernest W. Burgess (ed.): *Aging in Western Societies*. The University of Chicago Press: Chicago.

Foster, A.J. 1970. 'Housing and Welfare of the Aged' in: Sidney Sax (ed.): *The Aged in Australian Society*. Angus and Robertson Ltd: London.

Giddens, Anthony.1989. *Sociology*. Polity Press. U.K.

Gaur, Rajan and Kaur,Amarjot. 2004. 'A Socio-Gerontological Study of the Institutionalised and Non-Institutionalised Elderly Living in and Around Chandigarh' in: Kapoor A K and Kapoor S (ed.): *India's Elderly-A Multidisciplinary Dimension*. Mittal Publications, New Delhi.

Help Age India. 2003. Infovergix Technologies Limited.

Kart, Cary S. 1990. *The Realities of Aging: An introduction to Gerontology*. Allyn and Bacon: Boston.

Modi, Ishwar. 2001. *Ageing and Human Development: Global Perspective*. Rawat Publications: Jaipur and New Delhi.

Mohanty, R P. 2004. 'Ageing and the Aged-An Overview' in: Kapoor A K and Kapoor S (ed.): *India's Elderly-A Multidisciplinary Dimension*. Mittal Publications, New Delhi.

Muttagi, P.K. 1997. *Aging Issues and Old Age Care*. Classical Publishing Company, New Delhi.

Patil, R.B. 1999 'Problems of the Aged in Goa : Some Reflections', Samaja Shodhana, *Journal of the Mangalore Sociology Association*, 8 (2).

Research, Reference and Training Division. 2001. *India 2001*. Ministry of Information and Broadcasting Government of India, New Delhi.

Sachdeva, D.R.1993. *Social Welfare Administration in India*. Kitab Mahal, Allahabad.

Saguna, B. 2004. 'Status of the Elderly' in: Kapoor A K and Kapoor S (ed.): *India's Elderly-A Multidisciplinary Dimension*. Mittal Publications, New Delhi.

Sahu, Chaturbhuj. 1998. *Problems of Ageing among the Indian Tribes*. Sarup & Sons, New Delhi.

Singh, K P.2001. 'Agrarian Trends in an Agrarian State-A Case study of Punjab', *Guru Nanak Journal of Sociology*, 22(1).

Shankar, Jogan. 1992. *Social Problems and Welfare in India*. Ashish Publishing House. New Delhi.

Sharma, M L and Dak, T M. 1987. *Aging in India: challenge for the society*. Ajanta Publications, Delhi.

Sinikka Dixon, A L. 2001. 'Cross-Culturally Comparative Structural Constraints Affecting the Social Aspects of

Aging' in: Sharma,K L. *Indian Journal of Gerontology*, Quarterly Journal devoted to research on Ageing, 15(1-2). Rawat Publications: New Delhi.

Sivakumar, Damodaran.2001. 'Integration of Strategies for the Care of Older Persons: A Cross-Cultural Study'. in: Sharma, K L. *Indian Journal of Gerontology*, Quarterly Journal devoted to research on Ageing, 15(3-4). Rawat Publications, New Delhi.

Soodan, K S.1975. *Ageing in India*. Minerva Associates Publications, Calcutta.

Srivastava, R C. 1994. *The Problem of Old Age*. Classical Publishing, New Delhi.

Sundari, S. and Geetha, N. 1999 'The Aged in India: A Demographic Profile', *Indian Association of Social Science Institutions*, Quarterly Journal, 18(1).

Sinha, *A C*. 1992. *Senior Citizens of Meghalaya : A Study of the Problems of the Aged and Need for Social Intervention*. North Eastern Hill University, Shillong. (Mimiographed Report on a project sponsored by Ministry of Welfare Government of India, New Delhi).

Srivastava, S K and Agrawal, S. 2004. 'Effect of Family Structure of Degree of Loneliness and Mental Health of Urban Aged Persons' in: Kapoor A K and Kapoor S (ed.): *India's Elderly—A Multidisciplinary Dimension*. Mittal Publications, New Delhi.

Sundari, S. and Geetha, N.1999. 'The Aged in India: A Demographic Profile', *Indian Association of Social Science Institutions*, Quarterly Journal, 18(1).

Thakur, M K. 2002. 'Genetic Determinants of Aging: Prospects in the New Millenium', *Indian Journal of Gerontology*,16(1-2).

Townsend, Peter. 1964. *The Last Refuge*. Routledge and Kegan Paul, London.

Uplaonkar, Amba Rao. 1999. 'Problems of the Aged', *Samaja Shodhana, Journal of the Mangalore Sociology Association*, 8(2).

Yadav, J P. 2004. *Aged in India—The Struggle to Survive*. Vol.2. Anmol Publications, New Delhi.

ANNEXURE–I

PART A

Village Name: District Name

1. Name (in full): Mr/Mrs/Miss ________

No.	Question	Option	Code
2.	Age:	60-65 yrs	1
		65-70 yrs	2
		70-75 yrs	3
		75-80 yrs	4
		80-85 yrs	5
		90 above	6
3.	Sex:	Male	1
		Female	2
4.	Family type:	Nuclear	1
		Exended	2
		Joint	
		Others (specify)	4
5.	Marital status:	Married	1
		Unmarried	2
		Widowed	3
		Separated	4
		Divorced	5
		Remarried	6
6.	Religion :	Catholic	1
		Protestant	2
		Indigeneous religion	3
		Hindu	4
		Buddhism	5
		Islam	6
		others (specify)	7
7.	Educational qualification :	Illiterate	1
		Primary (CL I-V)	2

		Middle (CL VI- IX)	3
		Matriculation (CL X-XI)	4
		HSSLC (CL XII)	5
		Degree (BA, BSc, BCom)	6
		Post Graduate (MA, MSc, MCom)	7
		Research Work	8
		Professional	
8.	Occupation (last held)	Agricultural labourer	1
		Carpenter	2
		Daily wage earner	3
		Business	4
		Professional	5
		Others (specify)	6
9.	Community :	Khasi	1
		Jaintia	2
		Garo	3
		Bengali	4
		Nepali	5
		Others (specify)	6
10.	Family income:	<Rs 1000 pm	1
		Rs 1000- Rs 2500 pm	2
		Rs 2500- Rs 5000 pm	3
		Rs 5000- Rs 10,000 pm	4
		Rs 10,000- Rs 15,000 pm	5
		Rs 15,000- Rs 20,000 pm	6
		Rs 20,000 above	7

PART B
(Social Characteristics)

1.	Children:	yes	1
		no	2
2.	If yes, number of children:	male	Total
		female	
3.	children dependent: if yes, go to question no.6	yes	1
		no	2
4.	If no, occupation of children	Teacher	1
		Professional	2
		Business	3
		Agricultural labourer	4
		Others (specify)	5
5.	Monthly income of children		
		<Rs 1000 pm	1
		Rs 1000- Rs 2500 pm	2
		Rs 2500- Rs 5000 pm	3
		Rs 5000- Rs 10,000 pm	4
		Rs 10,000- Rs 15,000 pm	5
		Rs 15,000- Rs 20,000 pm	6
		Rs 20,000 above	7
6.	If yes, no. of dependents:	male	Total
		Female	
7.	manner of dependency:	student	1
		unemployed	2
		others(specify)	3
8.	any contacts with children living separately	yes	1
		no	2
9.	Reasons for leaving parents by the married children –	-due to service	1
		-due to business	2
		-others(specify)	3

10.	Feel lonely/ neglected/sad. If no go to question no.12	-yes	1
		-No	2
11.	If yes, reasons for loneliness:		
		- son/daughter is not staying with them	1
		- husband/wife died	2
		- others (specify)	3
12.	Whether do any household works?	-Yes	1
		-No	2
13.	If yes, who help in the household activities		
		-the elderly themselves	1
		-help other member in the household	2
		-others(specify)	3
14.	Who take more care-		
		-sons or daughters	1
		-both sons and daughters	2
		-others (specify)	3
15.	If no children, whether staying together with relatives. If no go to question no.17	-Yes	1
		-No	2
16.	If yes, please specify what sort of relation		
		-niece	1
		-nephew	2
		-granddaughter	3
		-grandson	4
		-cousin	5
		-others (specify)	6
17.	If no, reasons why not staying together-		
		-don't want	1
		-have own family	2
		-no contacts	3
		-others (specify)	4

18. What is the attitude of family members/relatives towards elderly

-see them with sympathy	1
-see them without sympathy	2
-bad mannered	3
-others (specify)	4

19. With whom are they staying and how are they treated

-good	1
-bad	2
others (specify)	3

20. Type of problem faced

-Financial	1
-Psychological	2
-Medical	3
-Physical	4
-others(specify)	5

21. Being a matrilineal society with strong traditional norms, customs and kinship ties, the status accorded to the elderly is usually high. Do you agree/disagree. Give reasons.

22. Whether neighbours are aware of their problems	-yes	1
	-No	2

23. Awareness about the longevity of the elderly people. On what basis

-live more than the past	1
-live less than the past	2
-live equal	3
-don't know	4

24. Perception about sex differential-

-higher for males	1
-higher for females	2
-equal for both	3

PART C
(Health Related Problems)

1. The general health condition of the elderly persons
   - -good 1
   - -bad 2

2. If bad, what kind of diseases suffered
   -Diabetes / Rheumatism / Gastric / Ulcer/ Heart disease/ Blood pressure / Paralysis /Asthma / Tuberculosis / Cannot see, hear, walk properly / Headache / Others (specify).

3. What is the type of treatment taken
   - -private doctor 1
   - -local medicine 2
   - -homeopathic 3
   - -allopathic 4
   - -government hospital/dispensary 5
   - -others(specify) 6

4. Reasons for not receiving treatment in the Government Clinic-
   - -hospital far away 1
   - -donot supply the proper medicine 2
   - -doctors donot attend them seriously 3
   - -do not receive well attention 4
   - -have to wait a long time 5

5. Whether required any personal assistance
   - -yes 1
   - -No 2

6. If yes, what type of assistance
   - -walking 1
   - -dressing 2
   - -bathing/bathroom 3
   - -others (specify) 4

7. If required, who gave assistance

-son	1
-daughter	2
-both	3
-relative	4
-others (specify)	5

8. Period of physical dependency or requiring personal attention from family members/relatives

<1 year	1
1-3 years	2
3-5 years	3
5-7 years	4
7-9 years	5
9 years above	6

PART- D
(Economic Characteristics)

1. Financially dependent and insecure

-yes	1
-no	2

2. if yes, period of financial dependency

<1 year	1
1-3 years	2
3-5 years	3
5-7 years	4
7-9 years	5
9 years above	6

3. On whom are they financially dependent

-son	1
-daughter	2
-relative	3
-others(specify)	4

4. Age of retirement from active life

50-55 years	1
55-60 years	2
60-65 years	3
65-70 years	4
70-75 years	5
75 years above	6

5. Reasons for retirement from active life

Due to sickness	1
Due to old age	2
Not allowed by family members/relatives	3
Others (specify)	4

6. Age of retirement from service for working persons
7. Whether still active after 60 years of age

-yes	1
-no	2

8. Whether received any pension or any other source of receiving financial assistance?

-yes	1
-no	2

PART E
(Recommendations)

1. What the society (headman/social workers or community workers/NGOs) think about the facilities that should be offered to the elderly.

2. Types of facilities-

-old age allowance	1
-government housing facility	2
-recreation facility	3
-health care services	4
-others (specify)	5

3. Type of Programs to be adopted for elderly-

-Social Security	1
-Recreation facilities	2
-Community's help	3
-Awareness of health education in the area	4
-others(specify)	5

4. Type of facilities to be adopted for those who have none to look after them

-Government housing	1
-Financial benefits	2
-Social help3	
-Facilities for health care services and Nursing	4
-Others (specify)	5

5. What should be done for sick elderly people-

-facilities for nursing in the home	1
-arrangement to take them to the hospital	2
-facilities for regular nursing	3
-facilities for health care services at home	4
-others(specify)	5

6. Opinions and suggestions of the elderly people that should be implemented for them.

NATIONAL POLICY ON OLDER PERSONS

Demographic Trends

1. Demographic ageing, a global phenomenon, has hit Indian shores as well. People are living longer. Expectation of life at birth for males has shown a steady rise from 42 years in 1951-60 to 58 years in 1986-90; it is projected to be 67 years in 2011-16, an increase of about 9 years in a twenty five year period (1986-90 to 2011-16). In the case of females, the increase in expectation of life has been higher- about 11 years during the same period, from 58 years in 1986-90 to 69 years in 2011-16. At age 60 too, the expectation of life shows a steady rise and is a little higher for women. In 1989-93, it was 15 years for males and 16 years for females.

2. Improved life expectancy has contributed to an increase in the number of persons 60+. From only 12 million persons 60+ in India in 1901, the number

crossed 20 million in 1951 and 57 million in 1991.Population projections for 1996-2016 made by the Technical Group on Population Projections (1996) indicate that the 100 million mark is expected to be reached in 2013. Projections beyond 2016 made by the United Nations (1996 revision) has indicated that India will have 108 million persons 60+ in 2030 and 326 million in 2050. The percentage of persons 60+ in the total population has seen a steady rise from 5.1 percent in 1901 to 6.8 percent in 1991. It is expected to reach 8.9 percent in 2016. Projections beyond 2016 made by United Nations (1996 revision) has indicated that 21 percent of the Indian population will be 60+ by 2050.

3. Growth rate on a larger demographic base implies a much larger increase in numbers. This will be the case in the coming years. The decade 2001-2011 is expected to witness an increase of 25 million persons 60+ which is equivalent to the total populations of persons 60+ in 1961. The twenty five year period 1991-2016 will witness an increase of 55.4 million persons 60+ which is nearly the same as the population of persons 60+ in 1991.In other words, in a twenty five year period starting 1991, the population 60+ will nearly double itself.

4. Sixty three per cent of the population in 1991 (36million) is in the age group 60-69 years, often referred to as 'young old' or 'not so old' while 11 per cent (6 million) is in the age group 80 years and over i.e in the 'older old' or 'very old' category. In 2016, the percentages in these age groups will be

almost the same, but the numbers are expected to be 69 million and 11 million respectively. In other words, close to six-tenths of the population 60-69 years can be expected to be in reasonably good physical and mental health, free of serious disability and capable of leading an active life. About one-third of the population 70-79 years can also be expected to be fit for a reasonably active life. This is indicative of the huge reserve of human resource.

5. Men outnumber women in India even after age 60 (29 million males, 27 million females 60+ in 1991). This will continue to be the situation in 2016 when there will be an estimated 57 million males and 56 million females 60+.

6. Incidence of widowhood is much higher among females 60+ than among males of the same age group because it is customary for women to get married to men older by several years; also, they do not remarry and live longer. There were in 1991, 14.8 million widowed females 60+ compared to 4.5 million widowed males. In other words, there were four times as many widowed females as widowed males.

Implications

7. The demographic ageing of population has implications at the macro and also at household level. The sheer magnitude of numbers is indicative both of the huge human reserve and also of the scale of endeavors necessary to provide social services and other benefits.

8. Demographic transition has been accompanied by changes in society and economy. These are of a positive nature in some areas and a cause of concern in others.

9. A growing number of persons 60+ in the coming decades will belong to the middle and upper income groups, be economically better off with some degree of financial security, have higher professional and educational qualifications, lead an active life in their 60s and even first half of the 70s, and have a positive frame of mind looking for opportunities for a more active, creative and satisfying life.

10. Some areas of concern in the situation of older persons will also emerge, signs of which are already evident, resulting in pressures and fissures in living arrangements of older persons. It is true that family ties in India are very strong and overwhelming majority lives with their sons or are supported by them. Also, working couples find the presence of old parents emotionally bonding and of great help in managing the household and caring for children. However, due to the operation of several forces, the position of a large number of older persons has become vulnerable due to which they cannot take for granted that their children will be able to look after them when they need care in old age, specially in view of the longer life span implying an extended period of dependency and higher costs to meet health and other needs.

11. Industrializations, urbanization, education and exposure to life styles in developed countries are

bringing changes in values and life styles. High cost of bringing up and educating children, and pressures for gratification of their desires affects transfer of share of income for the care of parents. Due to shortage of space in dwellings in urban areas and high rents, migrants prefer to leave their parents in their native place. Changing roles and expectations of women, their concepts of privacy and space, desire not to be encumbered by caring responsibilities of old people for long periods, career ambitions, and employment outside the home implies considerably reduced time for care giving. Also, adoption of small family norm by a growing number of people implies availability of fewer care givers, since in a growing number of families, daughters, too, are fully occupied, pursuing their educational or work career. The position of single persons, particularly females, is more vulnerable in old age as few persons are willing to take care of non-lineal relatives. So also is the situation of widows an overwhelming majority of whom have no independent source of income, do not own assets and are totally dependent.

The Mandate

12. Well-being of older persons has been mandated in the Constitution of India. Article 41, a Directive Principle of State Policy, has directed that the State shall, within the limits of its economic capacity and development, make effective provision for securing the right to public assistance in cases of old age. There are other provisions, too, which direct the

State to improve the quality of life of its citizens. Right to equality has been guaranteed by the Constitution as a Fundamental Right. These provisions apply equally to older persons. Social security has been made the concurrent responsibility of the Central and State Government.

13. The last two decades have witnessed considerable discussions and debate on the impact of demographic transition and of changes in society and economy on the situation of older persons. The United Nations Principles for Older Persons adopted by the United Nations General Assembly in 1991, the Proclamation on Ageing and the Global Targets on Ageing for the year 2001 adopted by the General Assembly in 1992, and various other Resolutions adopted from time to time, are intended to encourage governments to design their own policies and programme in this regard.

14. There has for several years been a demand for a Policy Statement by the State towards its senior citizens so that they do not face an identity crisis and know where they stand in their overall national perspective. The need has been expressed at different forums where ageing issues have been deliberated. The Statement, by indicating the principles underlying the policy, the directions, the needs that will be addressed and the relative roles of governmental and non-governmental institutions, is expected to facilitate carving out of respective areas of operation and action in the direction of a humane age integrated society.

II. NATIONAL POLICY STATEMENT

15. The National Policy seeks to assure older persons that their concerns are national concerns and they will not live unprotected, ignored or marginalized. The goal of the National Policy is the well-being of older persons. It aims to strengthen their legitimate place in society and help older persons to live the last phase of their life with purpose, dignity and peace.

16. The Policy visualizes that the State will extend support for financial security, health care, shelter, welfare and other needs of older persons, provide protection against abuse and exploitation, make available opportunities for development of the potential of older persons, seek their participation, and provide services so that they can improve the quality of their lives. The Policy is based on some broad principles.

17. The Policy recognizes the need for affirmative action in favour of the elderly. It has to be ensured that the rights of the older persons are not violated and they get opportunities and equitable share in development benefits. Different sectors of development, programmes and administrative actions will reflect sensitivity of older persons living in rural areas. Special attention will be necessary to older females so that they do not become victims of triple neglect and discrimination on account of gender, widowhood and age.

18. The Policy views the life cycle as a continuum, of

which post 60 phase of life is an integral part. It does not view age 60 as the cut off point for beginning a life of dependency. It considers 60+ as a phase when the individual should have the choices and the opportunities to lead an active, creative, productive and satisfying life. An important thrust is, therefore, on active and productive involvement of older persons and not just their care.

19. The Policy values an age integrated society. It will endeavour to strengthen integration between generations, facilitate two way flows and interactions, and strengthen bonds between the young and the old. It believes in the development of a social support system, informal as well as formal, so that the capacity of families to take care of older persons is strengthened and they can continue to live in their family.

20. The Policy recognizes that older persons, too, are a resource. They render useful services in the family and outside. They are not just consumers of goods and services but also their producers. Opportunities and facilities need to be provided so that they can continue to contribute more effectively to the family, community and society.

21. The Policy firmly believes in the empowerment of older persons so that they can acquire better control over their lives and participate in decision making on matters which affect them as well as on other issues as equal partner in the development process. The decision making process will seek to involve them to a much larger extent, as they constitute 12

per cent of the electorate, a proportion which will rise in the coming years.

22. The Policy recognizes that larger budgetary allocations from the State will be needed and the rural and urban poor will be given special attention. However, it is neither feasible nor desirable for the State alone to attain the objectives of the National Policy. Individuals, families, communities and institutions of civil society have to join hands as partners.

23. The Policy emphasizes the need for expansion of social and community services for older persons, particularly women, to enhance their accessibility and use by removing socio-cultural, economic and physical barriers and making the services client oriented and user friendly. Special efforts will be made to ensure that rural area, where more than three-fourths of the older population lives are adequately covered.

PRINCIPLE AREAS OF INTERVENTION AND ACTION STRATEGIES

Financial Security

24. A great anxiety in old age relates to financial insecurity. When the issue is seen in the context of fact that one-third of the population (1993-94) is below the poverty line and about one-third are above it but belong to the lower income group, the financial situation of the two-thirds of the population 60+ can be said to fragile. Some level of income security in old age is a goal which will be

given very high priority. Policy instruments to cover different income segments will be developed.

25. For elderly persons below the poverty line, old age pensions provide some succour. Coverage under the old age pension scheme for poor persons will be significantly expanded from the January 1997 level of 2.76 million with the ultimate objective of covering all older persons below the poverty line. Simultaneously, it will be necessary to prevent delays and check abuses in the matter of selection and disbursement. Rate of monthly pension will need to be revised at intervals so that inflation does not deflate its real purchasing power. Simultaneously, the public distribution system will reach out to cover all persons 60+ living below the poverty line.

26. Employees of government and quasi government bodies and industrial workers desire better returns from accumulations in provident funds through prudent and safe investment of the funds. Issues involved will be given careful consideration. It will be ensured that settlement of pension, provident fund, gratuity and other retirement benefits is made promptly and superannuated persons and not put to hardship due to administrative lapses. Accountability for delays will be fixed. Redress mechanism for superannuated persons will ensure prompt, fair and humane treatment. Widows will be given special consideration in the matter of settlement of benefits accruing to them on the demise of husband.

27. Pension is a much sought after income security scheme. The base of pension coverage needs to be considerably expanded. It would be necessary to facilitate the establishment of pension schemes both in the private as well as the public sector for self-employed and salaried persons in non-governmental employment, with provision for employers also to contribute. Paramount considerations in regard to pension schemes are total security, flexibility, liquidity and maximization of returns. Pension funds will function under the watchful eye of a strong regulatory authority which lays down the investment norms and provide strong safeguards.

28. Taxation policies will reflect sensibility to the financial problems of older persons which accelerate due to very high costs of medical and nursing care, transportation and support services needed at home. Organizations of senior citizens have been demanding a much higher standard deduction for them a standard annual rebate for medical treatment, whether domicile salary or hospital based, in cases where superannuated persons do not get medical coverage from their erstwhile employers. There are also demands that some tax relief must be given to son or daughter when old parents co-reside and also allow some tax rebate for medical expenses. These and other proposes of tax relief will be considered.

29. Long term savings installments will be promoted to reach both rural and urban areas. It will be

necessary for the contributors to feel assured that the payments at the end of the stipulated period are attractive enough to take care of the likely erosion in purchasing power due to erosion. Earners will be motivated to save in their active working years for financial security in old age.

30. Pre-retirement counseling programmes will be promoted and assisted.

31. Employment in income generating activities after superannuation should be the choice of the individual. Organizations which provide career guidance, training and orientation, and support services will be assisted. Programmes of non-governmental organizations for generating incomes of old persons will be encouraged. Age related discrimination in the matter of entitlement to credit; marketing and other facilities will be removed. Structural adjustment policies may affect the older workers in some sectors more adversely, especially those in household or small scale industry. Measures will be taken to protect their interests.

32. The right of parents without any means to be supported by their children having sufficient means has been recognized by Section 125 of the Criminal Procedure Code. The Hindu Adoptions and Maintenance Act, 1956, too secure this right to parents. To simplify the procedure, provide speedy relief, lay down the machinery for processing cases, and define the rights and circumstances in a comprehensive manner, the Himachal Pradesh

Legislative Assembly passed the Himachal Pradesh Maintenance of Parents and Dependents Bill, 1996. The Government of Maharashtra has prepared a Bill on similar lines. Other States will be encouraged to pass similar legislation so that old parents unable to maintain themselves do not face abandonment and acute neglect.

Health Care and Nutrition

33. With advancing age, old persons have to cope with health and associated problems some of which may be chronic, of a multiple nature require constant attention and carry the risk of disability and consequent loss of autonomy. Some health problems specially when accompanied by impaired functional capacity, require long term management of illness at home, and of nursing care.

34. Health care needs of older persons will be given high priority. The goal should be good affordable health services, very heavily subsidized for the poor and a graded system of users charges for others. It will be necessary to have a judicious mix of public health services, health insurance, health services provided by not for profit organizations including trusts and charities, and private medical care. While the first of these will require greater State participation, the second category will need to be promoted by the State, the third category given some assistance, concessions and relief and the fourth encouraged but subjected to some degree of regulations, preferably by an association of providers of private care.

35. The primary health care system will be the basic structure of public health care. It will strengthened and oriented to be able to meet the health care needs for older persons as well as public health services, preventive, curative, restorative and rehabilitative, will be considerably expanded and strengthened, and geriatric care facilities provided at secondary and tertiary levels. This will imply much larger public sector outlays, proper distribution of services in rural and urban areas, and much better health administration and delivery systems.

36. The development of health insurance will be given high priority to cater to the needs of different income segments of the population and have provision for varying contributions and benefits. Packages catering to the lower income groups will be entitled to state subsidy. Various relief and concessions will be given to health insurance to enlarge the base of coverage and make them affordable.

37. Trusts, charitable societies and voluntary agencies will be promoted, encouraged and assisted by way of grants, tax relief and land at subsided rates to provide free beds, medicines and treatment to the very poor elder citizens, and reasonable user charges for the rest of the population.

38. Private medical care has expanded in recent years offering the latest medical treatment facilities to those who can afford it. Where land and other facilities are provided at less than market rates, bodies representing private hospitals and nursing

homes will be requested to direct their members to offer a discount to older patients. Private general practitioners will be extended opportunities for orientation in geriatric care.

39. Public hospitals will be directed to ensure that elderly patients are not subjected to long waits and visits to different counters for medical tests and treatment. They will endeavour to provide separate counters and convenient timings on specified days. Geriatric wards will be set up.

40. Medical and paramedical personnel in primary, secondary and tertiary health care facilities will be given training and orientation in health care of the elderly. Facilities for specialization in geriatric medicine will be provided in the medical colleges. Training in nursing care will include geriatric care. Problems of accessibility and use of health services by the elderly arise due to distance absence of escort and transportation. Difficulties in reaching a public health care, family will be addressed through mobile health services, special camps and ambulances services by charitable institutions and not for profit health care organizations. Hospitals will be encouraged to have a separate Welfare Fund which will receive donations and grants for providing free treatment and medicines to poor elderly patient.

41. For the old who are chronically ill and are deprived of family support, hospices support or assisted by the State, public charity, and voluntary organizations will be necessary. These are also

needed to cater to cases of abandonment of chronically ill aged patients admitted to public hospitals.

42. Assistance will be given to geriatric care societies for the production and distribution of instruction material on self care by older persons. Preparation and distribution of easy to follow guidance material on health and nursing care of older persons for the use of family care givers will also be supported.

43. Older persons and their families will be given access to educational material on nutritional needs in old age. Information will be made available on the foods to avoid and the right foods to eat. Diet recipes suiting tastes of different regions which are nutritious, tasty, fit into the dietary pattern of the family and the community, are affordable and can be prepared from locally available vegetables, cereals and fruits, will be disseminated.

44. The concept of health ageing will be promoted. It is necessary to educate older persons and their families that diseases are not a corollary of advancing age nor is a particular chronological age the starting point for decline in health status. On the contrary, preventive health care and early diagnosis can keep a person in reasonably good health and prevent disability.

45. Health education programmes will be strengthened by making use of mass media, folk media and other communication channels which reach out to different segments of the population. The capacity

to cope with illness and manage domiciliary care will be strengthened. Programmes will also be developed targeting the younger and middle age groups to inform them how lifestyles during early years affect health status in later years. Messages on how to stay healthy for the entire life span will be given. The importance of balanced diets, physical exercise, regular habits, stress reduction, regular medical check-up, time for leisure and recreation, and pursuits of hobbies will be conveyed. Programmes on yoga, meditation and methods of relaxation will be developed and transmitted through different channels of communication to reach diverse audiences.

46. Mental health services will be expanded and strengthened. Families will be provided with counseling facilities and information on the care and treatment of older persons having mental health problems.

47. Non-governmental organizations will be encouraged and assisted through grants, training and orientation of their personnel, and various concessions and relief to provide ambulatory services, day care and health care to complement the efforts of the State.

Shelter

48. Shelter is a basic human need. The stock of housing for different income segments will be increased. Housing schemes for urban and rural lower income segments will earmark 10 per cent of the houses/

house sites for allotment to older persons. This will include Indira Awas Yojana and other schemes of the government. Earning persons will be motivated to invest in their housing in their earning days so that they have no problems of shelter when they grow old. This will require speedy urban land development for housing, time bound provision of civic services and communication links, availability of loans at reasonable rates, easy repayment installments, time-bound construction schedules and tax relief. Development of housing has to be a joint endeavour of public and private sectors and require participation of Housing Development Boards, civic authorities, housing finance institutions and private developers and builders. Older persons will be given easy access to loans for purchase of housing and for major repairs, with easy repayment schedules.

49. Layouts of housing colonies will have to respond to the lifestyles of the elderly. It will have to be ensured that there are no physical barriers to mobility, and accessibility to shopping complexes, community centers, parks and other services are safe and easy. A multi-purpose centre for older persons is a necessity for social interaction and to meet other needs. It will, therefore, be necessary to earmark sites for such centers in all housing colonies. Segregation of older persons in housing colonies has to be avoided as it prevents interaction with the rest of the community. Three or four storeyed houses without lifts are unfriendly to older persons,

tend to isolate them, restrain their movement outside the home, and are a serious barrier to access to services. Preferences will be given to older persons in the allotment of flats on the ground floor.

50. Group housing of older persons comprising flat lets with common service facilities for meals, laundry, common room and rest rooms will be encouraged. These would have easy access to community services, medicare, parks, recreation and cultural centers.

51. Education, training and orientation of town planners, architects and housing administrators will include modules on needs of older persons for safe and comfortable living.

52. Older persons and their families will be provided access to information on prevention of accidents and on measures which enhance safety, taking cognizance of reduced physical capacity and infirmities.

53. Noise and other forms of pollution affect children, the sick and older persons more adversely. Norms will be laid down and strictly enforced.

54. Civic authorities and bodies providing public utilities will be required to give top priority to attending complaints of older persons. Payment of civic dues will be facilitated. Older persons will be given special consideration in prompt dealing with matters relating to transfer of property, mutation, property tax and other matters. Harassment and abuses in such cases will be checked.

Education

55. Education, training and information needs of older persons will be met. These have received virtually no attention in the past. Information and educational materials relevant to the lives of older people will be developed and widely disseminated using mass media and non-formal communication channels.

56. Discriminations, if any, against older persons for availing opportunities for education, training and orientation will be removed. Continuing education programmes will be encouraged and supported. These would cover a wide spectrum ranging from career development to creative use of leisure, appreciation of art, culture and social heritage, and imparting skills in community work and welfare activities. Assistance of open universities will be sought to develop packages using distance learning techniques. Access of older persons to libraries of universities, research institutions and cultural centers will be facilitated.

57. Educational curriculum at all stages of formal education as also non-formal education programmes will incorporate material to strengthen intergenerational bonds and mutually supporting relationships. Interactions with the educational institutions will be facilitated whereby older persons with professional qualifications and knowledge in science, arts, environment, socio-cultural heritage, sports and other areas could interact with children and young persons. Schools

will be encouraged and assisted to develop outreach programmes for interacting with older persons on a regular basis, participate in the running of senior citizens centers and develop activities in them.

58. Individuals of all ages, families and communities will be provided with information about the ageing process and the changing roles, responsibilities and relationships at different stages of the life cycle. The contributions of older persons inside the household and outside will be highlighted through the media and other forums and negative images, myths and stereotypes dispelled.

Welfare

59. The main thrust of welfare will be to identify the more vulnerable among the older persons such as the poor, the disabled, the infirm, the chronically sick and those without family support, and provide welfare services to them on a priority basis. The policy will be to consider institutional care as the last resort when personal circumstances are such that stay in old age homes becomes absolutely necessary.

60. Non-institutional services by voluntary organizations will be promoted and assisted to strengthen the coping capacity of older persons and their families. This has become necessary since families, as they become smaller and women work outside the home, have to cope with scarcity of full time care givers. Support services will provide

some relief through sharing of the family's caring responsibilities.

61. Assistance will be provided to voluntary organizations by way of grants-in-aid for construction and maintenance of old age homes. Those for the poor will be heavily subsidized. It is important that such institutions become lively places of stay and provide opportunities to residents to interact with the outside world. Non-governmental organizations will be encouraged to seek professional expertise in the designing of old age homes, keeping in view needs of group living at this stage of the life cycle and the class of clients they serve. Minimum standards of services in such homes will be developed and facilities provided for training and orientation of persons employed in these homes.

62. Voluntary organizations will be encouraged and assisted to organize services such as day care, multi-service citizen's centers, reach out services, supply of disability related aids and appliances, assistance to old persons to learn to use them, short term stay services and friendly home visits by social workers. For old couples or persons living on their own, helpline, telephone assurance services, help in maintaining contacts with friends, relatives and neighbours and escorting older persons to hospital, shopping complexes and other places will be promoted for which assistance will be given to voluntary organizations. Older persons will be encouraged to form informal groups of their own in

the neighbourhood, which satisfy the needs for social interaction, recreation and other activities. For a group of neighbourhoods/villages, the formation of senior citizen's forums will be encouraged.

63. A Welfare Fund for older persons will be set up. It will obtain funding, support from government, corporate sector, trusts, charities, individual donors and others. Contributions to the Fund will be given tax relief. States will be expected to establish similar Funds.

64. The need for plurality of arrangements for welfare services is recognized. Government, voluntary organizations and private sector agencies all have a place, the latter catering to those who have the means and desire better standards of care.

Protection of Life and Property

65. Old persons have become soft targets for criminal elements. They also become victims of fraudulent dealings and of physical and emotional abuse within the household by family members to force them to part with their ownership rights. Widow's rights of inheritance, occupancy and disposal are at times violated by their own children and relatives. It is important that protection is available to older persons. The introduction of special provisions in IPC to protect older persons from domestic violence will be considered and machinery provided to attend all such cases promptly. Tenancy legislation will be reviewed so that the rights of occupancy of older persons are restored speedily.

66. Voluntary organizations and associations of older persons will be assisted to provide protective services and help to senior citizens through helpline services, legal aid and other measures.

67. Police will be directed to keep a friendly vigil on older couples or old single persons living alone and promote mechanisms of interaction with neighbourhood associations. Information and advice will be made available to older persons on the importance of keeping contacts on phone with relatives, friends and neighbours and on precautions to be taken on matters such as prevention of unauthorized entry, hiring of domestic help, visits of repair and maintenance persons, vendors and others, and the handling of cash and valuables.

Other Areas of Action

68. There are various other areas which would need affirmative action of the State to ensure that policies and programmes reflect sensitivity to older persons. Among these are issue of identity cards by the administration; fare concessions in all modes of travel; preference in reservation of seats and earmarking of seats in local public transport; modifications in designs of public transport vehicles for easy entry and exit; strict enforcement of traffic discipline and zebra crossings to facilitate older persons to cross streets, priority in gas and telephone connections and in fault repairs; removal of physical barriers to facilitate easy movement; concessions in entrance fees in leisure and

entertainment facilities, art and cultural centers, and places of tourist interest.

69. Speedy disposals of complaints of older persons relating to fraudulent dealings, cheating and other matters will go a long way in providing relief to them. Machinery for achieving this objective will be put in place.

70. Issues pertaining to older persons will be highlighted every year on the National Older Person's Day. The year 2000 will be declared as the National Year for Older Persons. Activities during the year will be planned and executed with the participation of different organizations.

71. Facilities, concessions and relief given to older persons by the Central and State governments and the agencies will be compiled, updated at regular intervals and made available to associations of older persons for wide dissemination.

Non-Governmental Organizations

72. The State alone cannot provide all the services needed by older persons. Private sector agencies cater to a small paying segment of the population. The National Policy recognizes the NGO sector as a very important institutional mechanism to provide user friendly affordable services to complement the endeavours of the State in this direction.

73. Voluntary effort will be promoted and supported in a big way and efforts made to remedy the current uneven spread both within a state and between states. There will be continuous dialogue and

communication with NGOs on ageing issues and on services to be provided. Networking, exchange of information and interactions among NGOs will be facilitated. Opportunities will be provided for orientation and training of manpower. Transparency, accountability, simplifications of procedures and timely release of grants to voluntary organizations will ensure better services. The grant-in-aid policy will provide incentives to encourage organizations to raise their own resources and not become dependent only on government funding for providing services on a sustainable basis.

74. Trusts, charities, religious and other endowments will be encouraged to expand their areas of concern to provide services to the elderly by involving them on ageing issues.

75. Older persons will be encouraged to organize themselves to provide services to fellow senior citizens thereby making use of their professional knowledge, expertise and contacts. Initiatives taken by them for advocacy, mobilization of public opinion, raising resources and community work will be supported.

76. Support will be provided for setting up volunteer programmes, which will mobilize the participation of older persons and others in community affairs interact with the elders and help them with their problems. Volunteers will be provided opportunities for training and orientation on handling problems of the elderly and kept abreast

of developments in the field to promote active ageing. Volunteers will be encouraged to assist the home bound elderly, particularly frail and elderly women and help them to overcome loneliness.

77. Trade unions, employers' organizations and professional bodies will be approached to organize sensitivity programmes for their members on ageing issues, and promote and organize services for superannuated workers.

Realizing the Potential

78. The National Policy recognizes that 60+ phase of life is a huge untapped resource. Facilities will be made available so that this potential is realized and individuals are enabled to make the appropriate choices.

79. Older persons, particularly women, perform useful but unsung roles in the household. Efforts will be made to make family members appreciate and respect the contribution of older persons in the running of the household especially when women, too, are working outside the home. Special programmes will be designed and disseminated through the media targeted at older persons so that they can enrich and update their knowledge, integrate tradition with contemporary needs and transmit more effectively socio-cultural heritage to the grandchildren.

Family

80. Family is the most cherished social institution in

India and the most vital non-formal social security for the old. Most of the older persons stay with one or more of their children, particularly when independent living is no longer feasible. It is for them the most preferred living arrangement and also the most emotionally satisfying. It is important that the familial support system continues to be functional and the ability of the family to discharge its caring responsibilities is strengthened through support services.

81. Programmes will be developed to promote family valued sensitize the young on the necessity and desirability of inter-generational bonding and continuity and the desirability of meeting filial obligations. Values of caring and sharing need to be reinforced. Society will need to be sensitized to accept the role of married daughters in sharing the responsibility of supporting older parents in the light of changing context where parents have only one or two children, in some situations only daughter. This would require some adjustment and changes in perceptions of in-laws in regard to sharing of caring responsibilities by sons and daughters as corollary to equal rights of inheritance and the greater emotional attachment that daughters have with their parents.

82. State policies will encourage children to co-reside with their parents by providing tax relief, allowing for medical expenses and giving preference in the allotment of houses. Persons will be encouraged to go in for long term savings instruments and health

insurance during their earning days so that financial load on families can be eased. NGOs will be encouraged and assisted to provide services which reach out to older persons in the home or in the community. Short term stay-in facilities for older persons will be supported so that families can get some relief when they go out. Counselling services will be strengthened to resolve intra-familial stresses.

Research

83. The importance of a good data base on older persons is recognized. Research activity on ageing will require to be strengthened. Universities, medical colleges and research institutions will be assisted to set up centers for gerontological studies and geriatrics. Corporate bodies, Bank Trusts and Endowments will be requested to institute chairs in Universities and medical colleges in gerontology and geriatrics. Funding support will be provided to academic bodies for research projects on ageing. Superannuated scientists will be assisted so that their professional knowledge can be utilized.

84. An interdisciplinary coordinating body on research will be set up. Data collecting agencies will be requested to have a separate age category 60 years and above. Professional associations of gerontologists will be assisted to strengthen research activity, disseminate research findings and provide a platform for dialogue, discussion, debate and exchange of information.

85. The necessity of a national institute of research, training and documentation is recognized. Assistance will be given for setting up resource centers in different parts of the country.

Training of Manpower

86. The Policy recognizes the importance of trained manpower. Medical colleges will be assisted to offer specialization in geriatrics. Training institutions for nurses and for the paramedical personnel need to introduce specific courses on geriatric care in their educational and training curriculum. In-service training centers will be strengthened to take up orientation courses on geriatric care. Assistance will be provided for development of curriculum and course material. Schools of Social Work and University Departments need to give more attention in their curriculum to issues relating to older persons, intervention strategies and organization of services for them. Facilities will be provided and assistance given for training and orientation of personnel of non-governmental organizations providing services to older persons. Exchange of training personnel will be facilitated.

87. Assistance will be given for development and organization of sensitization programmes on ageing for legislative, judicial and executive wings at different levels.

Media

88. The National Policy recognizes that media have a very important role to play in highlighting the

changing situation of older persons and in identifying emerging issues and areas of action. Creative use of media can promote the concept of active ageing and help dispel stereotypes and negative images about this stage of life cycle. Media can also help to strengthen inter-generational bonds and provide individuals, families and groups with information and educational material which will give better understanding of the ageing process and of ways to handle problems as they arise.

89. The Policy aims to involve mass media as well as informal and traditional communication channels on ageing issues. It is necessary to provide opportunities to media personnel to have access to information apart from their own independent sources of information and reporting of field situations. Their participation in orientation programmes on ageing will be facilitated. Opportunities will be extended for greater interaction between media personnel and persons active in the field of ageing.

III. IMPLEMENTATION

90. The National Policy on Older Persons will be very widely disseminated for which an action plan will be prepared so that its features remain in constant public focus.

91 The Policy will make a change in the lives of senior citizens only if it is implemented. While the government and its principal organs has some basic responsibilities in the matter, other institutions as

well as individuals will need to consider how they can play their respective roles for the well-being of older persons. Collaborative action will go a long way in achieving a more humane society which gives older persons their legitimate place. Apex level organizations of older persons have special responsibilities in this regard so that they can function as a watchdog, energize continuing action, mobilize public opinion and generate pressure for implementation of the Policy.

92. The Ministry of Social Justice and Empowerment will be the nodal Ministry to coordinate all matters relating to the implementation of the Policy. A separate Bureau of Older Persons will be set up. An Inter-Ministerial Committee will coordinate matters relating to implementation of the National Policy and monitor its progress. States will be encouraged to set up separate Directorate of Older Persons and set up machinery for coordination and monitoring.

93. Five Year and Annual Action Plans will be prepared by each Ministry to implement aspects which concern them. These will indicate steps to be taken to ensure flow of benefits to older persons from general programmes and from schemes specially formulated for their wellbeing. Targets will be set within the framework of a time schedule. Responsibility for implementation of action points will be specified. The Planning Commission and the Finance Ministry will facilitate budgetary provisions required for implementation. The Annual

Report of each Ministry will indicate progress achieved during the year.

94. Every three years, a detailed review will be prepared by the nodal Ministry on the implementation of the National Policy. There will be non-official participation in the preparation of the document. The review will be a public document. It will be discussed in a National Convention. State Governments and Union Territory Administrations will be urged to take similar action.

95. An autonomous National Council for Older persons headed by the Minister for Social Justice & Empowerment will be set up to promote and co-ordinate the concerns of older persons. The Council will include representatives of relevant Central Ministries and the Planning Commission. Five States will be represented on the Council of rotation. Adequate representation will be given to non-official members representing Non-Government Organizations, Academic Bodies, Media and experts on ageing issues from different fields.

96. An autonomous registered National Association of Older Persons (NAOPS) will be established to mobilize senior citizens, articulate their interests, promote and undertake programmes and activities for their well being and to advise the Government on all matters relating to Older Persons. The Association will have National. State and District level offices and will choose its own office bearers. The Government will provide financial support to

establish the National and State level Offices while the District level Offices will be established by the Association from its own resources which may be raised through Membership subscriptions, donations, and other admissible means. The Government will also provide financial assistance to the National and State level Offices to cover both recurring as well as non-recurring administrative costs for a period of 15 years and thereafter the Association is to be expected to be financially self-sufficient.

97. Panchayati Raj institutions will be encouraged to participate in the implementation of the National Policy, address local level issues and needs of the ageing and implement programmes for them. They will provide Forums for discussing concerns of older persons and activities that need to be taken. Such forums will be encouraged at panchayat, block and district level. They will have adequate representation of older women. Panchayats will mobilize the talents and skills of older persons and draw up plans for utilizing these at the local level. Amongst others, the help of the Social Justice Committees of the village panchayats will be taken to advocate different measures for giving effect to the policy.

98. In order to ensure effective implementation of the policy at different levels, from time to time the helps of experts of public administration shall be taken to prepare the details of the organizational set up for the implementation, coordination and monitoring of the policy.

ANNEXURE–III

NATIONAL PROGRAMMES FOR CARE OF OLDER PERSONS : An Update*

Demographic ageing is a global phenomenon. With a comparatively young population, India is still poised to become home to the second largest number of older persons in the world. Projection studies indicate that the number of 60+ in India will increase to 100 million in 2013 and to 198 million in 2030. The special features of the elderly population in India are :- (a) a majority (80%) of them is in the rural areas, thus making service delivery a challenge, (b) feminization of the elderly population (51% of the elderly population would be women by the year 2016) , (c) increase in the number of the older-old (persons above 80 years) and (d) a large percentage (30%) of the elderly are below poverty line.

*Source: Ministry of Social Justice & Empowerment website

Social Defence Division, under the Ministry for Social Justice and Empowerment, provides for the need of care for the older persons through its various programmes and initiatives.

National Policy for Older Persons

The National Policy for Older Persons (NPOP) was announced in January, 1999, with the primary objective viz. to encourage individuals to make provision for their own as well as their spouse's old age; to encourage families to take care of their older family members; to enable and support voluntary and non-governmental organizations to supplement the care provided by the family; to provide care and protection to the vulnerable elderly people, to provide health care facility to the elderly; to promote research and training facilities to train geriatric care givers and organizers of services for the elderly; and to create awareness regarding elderly persons to develop themselves into fully independent citizens.

Steps already taken for implementation of NPOP

The Government has re-constituted the National Council for Older Persons (NCOP) in 2005 under the Chairpersonship of Minister for Social Justice and Empowerment to advise and aid the Government on policies and programmes for older persons and also to provide feedback to the Government on the implementation of the National Policy on Older Persons as well as on specific programme initiatives for older persons. The NCOP is the highest body to advice and coordinate with the Government in the formulation and implementation of policy and programmes for the welfare of the aged.

The present number of NCOP members is 41. The NCOP members are experienced and well known individuals representing NGOs, citizens' groups, retired persons' associations and other walks of life, such as law, social welfare and security, research and medicine. The council is engaged in several issues concerning the welfare and care of the older persons. A few of these issues are as follows:

Uniform age of 60+ for extending facilities/ benefits to senior citizens;

Financial security to the elderly population by: (1) Proposing tax benefits and higher interest rates for senior citizens (2) Promotion of long term savings in both rural and urban areas (3) Increased coverage and revision of old age pension schemes for the destitute elderly and (4) Prompt settlement of pension, provident fund, gratuity and other retirement benefits;

Health care and nutritional needs of the elderly populations by: (1) Strengthening of primary health care system to enable it to meet the health care needs of older persons; (2) Training and orientation to medical and para medical personnel in health care of the elderly. (3) Promotion of the concept of healthy ageing. (4) Assistance to societies for production and distribution of material on geriatric care. (5) Provision of separate queues and reservation of beds for elderly patients.

Food security and shelter by: (1) Coverage under the Antyodaya Scheme to be increased with emphasis on provisions for the benefit of older persons especially the destitute and marginalized sections. (2) Earmarking ten percent of houses/house sites for allotment to older persons. (3) Barrier-free environment for the disabled and elderly persons etc.

Meeting the education, training and information needs of older persons.

Identification of the most vulnerable among the older persons and working for their welfare.

Realizing the crucial role by the media in highlighting the situation of older persons and emphasising their continued role in Society

Protection of life and property of the elderly population.

Inter-Ministerial Committee

The Ministry has also set up Inter-Ministerial Committee (IMC) headed by Secretary (SJ & E) for ensuring speedy implementation of the decisions taken in the meeting of the National Council for Older Persons and also to review the progress of plan of action for implementation by the concerned Ministries/ Departments as in many cases, the activities have to be initiated by the other Ministries/ Departments and, therefore, a combined effort by all the Ministries/ Departments is required to implement the National Policy on Older Persons. The Inter-Ministerial Committee comprises of 22 Ministries/Departments and representatives of State Governments and UT Administrations. The Inter-Ministerial Committee is responsible for the implementation of the action points as described.

SCHEMES

An Integrated Programme for Older Persons

Under this scheme financial assistance up to 90 per cent of the project cost is provided to NGOs for establishing and maintaining old age homes, day care centers, mobile medicare units and to provide non-institutional services to older persons. The scheme has been made flexible so as to meet the diverse needs of older persons, including reinforcement and strengthening of the family, awareness generation on issues pertaining to older persons, popularisation of the concept of life long preparation for old age, facilitating productive ageing, etc.

Scheme of Assistance to Panchayati Raj Institutions/ VOs/SHGs

Scheme of Assistance to Panchayati Raj Institutions/ Voluntary Organisations/Self Help Groups for Construction of old age homes/multi service centres for older persons. This scheme provides for one time construction grant for old age homes/multi service centers. The registered societies, public trust, Charitable Companies or registered Self-help Groups of Older Persons in addition to Panchayati Raj Institutions are eligible to get the assistance under this scheme.

New Initiatives

In recent times, the society is witnessing a gradual but definite withering of joint family system. As a result, a large number of parents is not being maintained by their children as was the normal social practice. They face many problems in the absence of adequate social security. Therefore, the Ministry of Social Justice and Empowerment has proposed law for promoting the maintenance, care and protection of older persons. The proposed legislation envisages setting up of Tribunal headed by Sub divisional magistrate in each district to deal with the maintenance claims of the parents. It has also mooted through legislation to lay down directions to the State governments/UT administrations to provide adequate medical facilities to older persons and take steps to ensure protection of their life and property.

The Ministry is also interacting with the State governments to bring about a uniformity of age for both male and female for the purpose of distribution of old age pension. Some States like Goa, Tripura and Karnataka have prepared State Policy and plan of action for the elderly people.

INDEX

A

Ageing, 1, 67, 93
Annapurna Scheme, 79
Atal Yogesh, 2

B

Baghmara, 21, 78, 84
Bali, Arun, 12
BDO , 80
BPL, 76, 77, 79, 91, 102, 106

C

Charitable organisations, 81
Children (of elderly),
  reasons for leaving parents by, 51
China, 6
Collins Dictionary of Sociology, 8
Community Workers, 85

D

Dependency,
  manner of, 49
Desjarlais, 2
Directive Principles, 7, 94
District Social Welfare, 77, 78
DRDA, 76, 77, 79
Drop-In Centre, 85

E

East Khasi Hills, 31, 34
  growth rate of elderly population in , 31, 32
Education department, 80
Elderly population, 1
  global scenario, 2
  Indian scenario, 5
  institutional and policy support to, xxxi, 106
  psychological support to, xxx, 105
  trends in financial dependency of, xxvii
  trends in growth of , xix
  trends in health status, xxii

trends in informal care giving to, xxvi
trends in psychological status, xxv
see also Elderly

Elderly,
attitude of family members towards, 53
educational qualification, 38
financial dependence of, 58
general health condition of, 68
health status of, 42, 44, 67-74
income, 39
living arrangement of, 54
loneliness, 51
meaning, 8
no. of dependent children, 48
occupation, 39
occupation of children, of 49
opinions of on care and support system, 89
problems, 10, 56
psychological status, 44
socioeconomic status, 96
social concerns for, 75-92
total no. of children of, 47
treatment to, 54 - 55

F

Financial dependence, 59

G

General information and status (of elderly), 36 - 45
age, 37
family type, 37
sex ratio, 37

Goa, 162

Government of Meghalaya, 75,77, 102

H

Health Care services, xxix, 99, 104

I

India, 5, 37

Indian family system, 11

Informal care givers,
and welfare of olderly, 46

Impulse Network-Shillong, 83

Integrated Programme for Older Persons, 7

IYOP, 4, 5

J

Jaintia Hills, 34

Jowai, 22, 84

K

Kapoor, 2

Karnataka, 102

Key informants, 15, 77

Kripa Foundation, 84

L

Legare, 3

Loneliness,
and neglect, 51
reasons for, 51

Longevity, awareness about, 56

M

Marital status, 38

Matrilineal tradition, 94

Meghalaya, xviii, 7, 92, 94, 96, 97

elderly persons in, 23
location, 18
natural resources, 19
population, xviii, 19
Mercy Home- Shillong, 81
Missionaries of Charity, 81
Modi, 7, 8
Mohanty, 8
MPAD, 83
MSJE, 7, 94

N

National Policy on Elder Persons, 7, 123-156
National Programmes for Care of Older Persons, 157 - 162
NGOs, 53, 86, 87, 88, 89
NOAPS, 76, 94, 102
Nongpoh, 22, 78
Nongstoin, 22

O

Off-farm activities, 49
Old Age Homes, 107
Old Age Pension, 82, 84, 85
see also NOAPS
Old age, xii,
financial security status, 40
security, xxviii, 103
trends in financial status, xx

P

Personal assistance, 70, 71
Present Study (the)
conclusion, 93-108
data collections, 16
objectives of, 14
methodology, 15

R

Role (of elderly)
erosion, 12
expectation. 13
isolation, 13
overload, 12

S

Sahu, 8
Shankar, 9
Shillong, 20, 77, 80, 84
Singh, 7
Social security measures, 101
Social Workers, 84
St. Saviour Society of Jesus Christ, 82
Suguna, 10
Sunderi, 6, 7

T

Thakur, 2, 6
Treatment
types of ,69
Tripura, 162
Tura, 20 ,78

U

United Nations Principles for Older Persons, 4
United Nations, 2, 4, 5, 6, 9,

W

West Garo Hills, 32, 33, 34
Williamnagar, 21, 79